Table of Contents

I0439085

Table of Contents

Section 1

Introduction and How To Use the Energy Savings Plus Health Guide

Purpose

The U.S. Environmental Protection Agency (EPA) developed the Energy Savings Plus Health Guide to protect and improve indoor air quality (IAQ) in schools during building upgrades, particularly energy efficiency upgrades and building renovation activities. Energy management and protection of IAQ both should be critical priorities for school facility management. As school districts pursue energy cost savings and occupant health-protection goals, there can be a mistaken impression that the two goals are at odds with each other. In fact, when energy efficiency and IAQ protection goals are integrated and addressed holistically, schools can achieve strong results in both areas. Alternatively, if careful attention is not paid to the interaction between energy management and IAQ, occupant health can suffer.

Background

A school's indoor environment can have a significant impact on health and learning. Children, in particular, are more vulnerable to the negative health and performance effects of poor environmental conditions, including IAQ. Children often are more heavily exposed to toxic substances in the environment than adults because they spend more time on the ground and engage in more hand-to-mouth behavior. Children also breathe more air, drink more water, and eat more food per pound of body weight than adults (American Academy of Pediatrics Council on Environmental Health, 2003). A child's respiratory, immune, nervous, reproductive, and skeletal systems continue to develop throughout childhood. Exposures to environmental contaminants that occur early in life can cause adverse health impacts in children that can have implications well into adulthood (EPA Office of Research and Development, 2007). Furthermore, some children with disabilities face unique challenges that might make them particularly vulnerable to the effects of an unhealthy school environment (EPA State School Environmental Health Guidelines, 2012). Examples of symptoms caused by poor IAQ include respiratory irritation, sore throat, asthma attacks, drowsiness, headaches and inability to concentrate.

Studies demonstrate associations between IAQ and the health and performance of students and staff members in U.S. schools. The research linking poor IAQ to children's health problems and reduced academic performance shows the critical role that a school's indoor environment plays in student achievement. For example, good physical conditions in the school and adequate outdoor air ventilation can reduce absenteeism and improve test scores. For more information, examples and supporting references, see the section of this Guide entitled *The Business Case for Integrating Energy Efficiency and IAQ.*

It is important to incorporate best practices for healthy and sustainable schools into energy efficiency upgrades and building renovation activities at schools. Schools can benefit, from both fiscal and facility management standpoints, by taking advantage of the complementary nature of many IAQ and energy-efficient building practices. Integrating energy efficiency and IAQ improvements—whether they involve the building structure, equipment or ongoing maintenance and operations—helps to streamline facility management and saves staff members' time. Typically, many of the same personnel are involved in planning and implementing energy efficiency and IAQ programs at schools. School energy managers, facility managers and IAQ coordinators should work together throughout the entire building upgrade process, from the design phases through construction and occupancy.

Energy management and protection of IAQ both should be critical priorities for school facility management. As school districts pursue energy cost savings and occupant health-protection goals, there can be a mistaken impression that the two goals are at odds with one another. In fact, when energy efficiency and IAQ protection goals are integrated and addressed holistically, schools can achieve strong results in both areas. Alternatively, if careful attention is not paid to the interaction between energy management and IAQ, occupant health can suffer. Energy management activities can disturb hazardous materials, such as asbestos, lead and polychlorinated biphenyls (PCBs); create dust; introduce new contaminants and contaminant pathways; create or aggravate moisture problems; and result in inadequate ventilation in occupied spaces.

This Guide focuses primarily on opportunities to protect and improve IAQ during building upgrades by preventing and controlling exposure of occupants to contaminants that may be disturbed or introduced during upgrade projects, controlling moisture, and ensuring that occupants are provided with adequate ventilation to promote health and comfort. This Guide does not (1) set new EPA regulatory requirements or in any way modify or supersede existing EPA regulatory requirements, (2) provide guidance on diagnosing occupant health problems or building-related illness, (3) address emerging issues that have not been linked to adverse health effects, (4) make training or training documents unnecessary, (5) provide detailed implementation guidance on how to achieve the intent of each recommendation in all situations, (6) identify funding availability or which programmatic funding sources should be used, or (7) provide guidance for prioritizing building-specific projects during the upgrade process. Portions of this

Important Basic Considerations for Protecting IAQ During Building Upgrades

Several energy retrofit and building upgrade activities can cause or aggravate IAQ problems as described in detail throughout this publication; however, **these important basic considerations must always be kept in mind:**

- **Occupants' and workers' exposure to airborne contaminants generated during and after energy retrofits and building upgrades activities should be minimized.**

Energy retrofits and other building upgrades can disturb existing contaminants known to cause health problems. Some of these contaminants have specific regulatory requirements (e.g., asbestos, lead) that must be followed.

- **Reducing air leakage across the building envelope should not be performed without ensuring that there will be adequate venting of combustion appliances and outdoor air ventilation to dilute and remove pollutants from within the building after the project is completed.**

Modifications that increase the airtightness of a building's envelope increase the potential for elevated levels of contaminants indoors. Care must always be taken to ensure that these activities do not cause improper venting of combustion appliances and increase occupant exposure to combustion by-products, including carbon monoxide; introduce increased indoor exposures to other pollutants, including radon; or introduce or exacerbate moisture and mold problems within the school.

- Providing adequate outdoor air ventilation.
- Providing filtration and air cleaning to supplement pollutant source control and ventilation.
- Protecting building elements, occupants and workers during construction projects.
- Ensuring that there is a strong communications plan in place to share the project's IAQ goals with occupants and other stakeholders, with a clear process for addressing feedback and concerns. This includes, for example, ensuring that building occupants are aware of the availability of the Asbestos Hazard Emergency Response Act (AHERA) Management Plan, Lead Safety Plan and Material Safety Data Sheets.
- Educating building occupants about the actions they can take to protect IAQ in their school.

The following references provide expanded information on these principles and may be valuable resources for users of this Guide:

- **EPA:** *IAQ Tools for Schools* Action Kit, http://www.epa.gov/iaq/schools/actionkit.html.
- **EPA:** *IAQ Design Tools for Schools*, http://www.epa.gov/iaq/schooldesign/index.html.
- **EPA:** Energy Star® *Building Upgrade Manual* (2008), http://www.energystar.gov/ia/business/EPA_BUM_Full.pdf?77f4-4b9b.
- **EPA:** *Moisture Control Guidance for Building Design, Construction and Maintenance* (2013), http://www.epa.gov/iaq/pdfs/moisture-control.pdf.
- **American Society of Heating, Refrigeration and Air Conditioning Engineers, Inc. (ASHRAE):** *Indoor Air Quality Guide: Best Practices for Design, Construction and Commissioning* (2009), http://iaq.ashrae.org/.

States and school districts interested in advancing this Energy Savings Plus Health Guide for their K–12 school systems can convene cross-disciplinary work groups of education, health, environmental and energy representatives to develop state-specific guidance, including available incentives or reimbursements. A recent report published by the Lawrence Berkeley National Laboratory, *Financing Energy Upgrades for K–12 School Districts: A Guide to Tapping into Funding for Energy Efficiency and Renewable Energy Improvements* (Borgeson and Zimring, 2013), can also be used as a resource.

Guide summarize certain regulatory requirements, but the requirements themselves, not the summaries in this Guide, govern.

Fundamental Principles of IAQ

The guidelines in this document are intended to encourage IAQ professionals to integrate health protections into energy efficiency and building renovation projects by undertaking the following activities:

- Integrating strong IAQ protections into the design, renovation and construction processes.
- Commissioning key energy and IAQ systems to ensure that they operate as designed.
- Controlling moisture in building assemblies, mechanical systems and occupied spaces.
- Limiting entry of contaminants from outdoors.
- Limiting contaminants from indoor sources.
- Capturing and exhausting contaminants from building equipment and activities.

How the Energy Savings Plus Health Guide Is Organized

The Energy Savings Plus Health Guide covers 23 specific priority issues and addresses common contaminants associated with building upgrades and critical building systems that affect IAQ. Each topic is organized in three sections:

Assessment Protocols: Measures to identify potential IAQ concerns in schools undergoing building upgrades.

Minimum Actions: Critical actions intended to correct deficiencies identified during the assessments, include minimum IAQ protections, and ensure that work does not cause or worsen IAQ or safety problems for occupants or workers (i.e., "Do No Harm"). Some of the Minimum Actions identified overlap with regulatory requirements but not all regulatory requirements are listed; others are recommendations for additional steps to protect and improve IAQ during building upgrades. Applicable regulatory requirements must be followed and the regulations, not the summaries in this Guide, establish the applicable requirements. Recommended steps are not mandatory.

Expanded Actions: Additional actions to promote healthy indoor environments that can be taken during building upgrades. EPA recommends considering these improvements when feasible and sufficient resources exist.

The Assessment Protocols, Minimum Actions and Expanded Actions are designed to incorporate good IAQ practices into a variety of energy efficiency and other building upgrade projects. To be effective, the recommended protocols and actions should be built into the earliest stages of project conceptualization and design. Working as a team, energy managers, facility managers, IAQ coordinators and risk managers can use the guidelines to better understand the interrelationships between energy efficiency and IAQ goals and identify opportunities available during typical energy management tasks to protect and promote healthy indoor environments.

Relevant standards and guidance documents for each priority issue are provided in an abbreviated format. More detailed information can be found in the References section.

The following icons are used in the Energy Savings Plus Health Guide:

 Indicates an issue that references **Appendix B: Communication and Education** for additional information and important considerations before, during and after the project is complete.

 Indicates an opportunity to communicate important messages via a sign or placard in the building; this symbol is used exclusively in Appendix B.

 Indicates an issue that references **Appendix C: Worker Protection** for recommended actions and additional resources to minimize health and safety risks for workers performing the building upgrades.

How To Use the Energy Savings Plus Health Guide

The entire **Energy Savings Plus Health Guide** can be used as a comprehensive resource. To streamline usability, examples of typical school energy efficiency and building upgrade projects are identified in Table 1. The following approach is suggested:

1. Use Table 1 to identify the type(s) of energy upgrade and other building renovation work being considered.

2. Use Table 1 to review IAQ/health risks and opportunities that may be encountered.

3. Use the "*Energy Saving Plus Health Checklist Generator*" tool, a Microsoft Excel file, to develop a customized verification checklist, along with the specific assessment protocols and recommended actions, tailored to the project.

Note: When using the "Energy Saving Plus Health Checklist Generator," it may be necessary to enable macros for functionality, depending on the user's Excel settings.

1. Identify Your Project(s)	2. Review IAQ/Health Risks and Opportunities	3. Use the "*Energy Saving Plus Health Checklist Generator*" to **Create Your Custom Verification Checklist, Assessment Protocols and Recommended Actions**

Examples of Projects With Energy Savings Plus Health Objectives	**Examples of IAQ/Health Risks and Opportunities**	**Potentially Applicable Priority Issues**

Table 1: Examples of School Energy Efficiency and Upgrade Projects

Examples of Projects With Energy Savings Plus Health Objectives	Examples of IAQ/Health Risks and Opportunities	Potentially Applicable Priority Issues
LIGHTING		
Lighting Upgrades • De-lamping: Removing unnecessary light bulbs/fixtures to save energy • Re-lamping: Replacing and cleaning lighting components and fixtures • Upgrading ballasts • Other modifications or upgrades (e.g., fixture lenses, specular reflectors, occupancy sensors)	**IAQ/Health Risks** • Asbestos-containing material, lead paint or PCBs may be disturbed during lighting replacement. PCBs may be present in older florescent light ballasts that are not labeled "No PCBs" or "electronic." • Mercury vapor or mercury-containing powder from broken fluorescent bulbs or improper use of drum-top crushers may be present. • Lighting upgrades likely will reduce sensible heat loads, which may affect moisture removal performance of the HVAC system. **Opportunities** • Remove and replace old fixtures containing hazardous materials with those that contain less hazardous materials. • Properly dispose of lamps containing mercury and fixtures containing PCBs.	1.0 Project Planning/Integrated Design 2.0 Commissioning 4.0 Asbestos 5.0 Lead 6.0 PCBs 13.0 Building Products/Materials Emissions 18.0 HVAC Equipment 21.0 Building Safety for Children and Other Occupants 22.0 Protecting IAQ During Construction 23.0 Jobsite Safety
BUILDING ENVELOPE		
Roof and Ceiling Assemblies • Repairing or replacing the roof • Upgrading roof and ceiling insulation • Upgrading moisture protection • Upgrading air sealing	**IAQ/Health Risks** • Asbestos-containing material, lead paint, PCBs or mold may be disturbed. • Installing spray-polyurethane foam may generate indoor contaminants. • Moisture may be trapped behind spray foam insulation when installed under a low pitch wooden roof deck, creating the potential for hidden, structural roof damage and mold. • Moisture may be trapped in insulation installed below drainage planes, vapor barriers or roof membranes (in cold climates). • Sealing the building envelope may increase levels of indoor contaminants, including radon, combustion by-products, moisture and mold, and volatile organic compounds (VOCs). Adequate ventilation must be provided to dilute and remove indoor pollutants. Radon mitigation systems may become necessary. **Opportunities** • Control for moisture by selecting moisture-resistant insulation, properly installing insulation materials, and ensuring surfaces and assemblies with condensation potential are properly sealed and insulated to avoid dew-point conditions. • Seal unwanted openings and leaks in the building envelope to reduce infiltration and conditions conducive to pest entry.	1.0 Project Planning/Integrated Design 2.0 Commissioning 3.0 Moisture Control and Mold 4.0 Asbestos 5.0 Lead 6.0 PCBs 7.0 Radon 8.0 Belowground Vapor-Forming Contaminants 9.0 Vehicle Exhaust 11.0 Pests 13.0 Building Products/Materials Emissions 14.0 Vented Combustion Appliances 15.0 Unvented Combustion Appliances 18.0 HVAC Equipment 19.0 Outdoor Air Ventilation 20.0 Exhaust Ventilation 21.0 Building Safety for Children and Other Occupants 22.0 Protecting IAQ During Construction 23.0 Jobsite Safety

Table 1: Examples of School Energy Efficiency and Upgrade Projects (continued)

Examples of Projects With Energy Savings Plus Health Objectives	Examples of IAQ/Health Risks and Opportunities	Potentially Applicable Priority Issues
Wall Assemblies • Repairing and sealing wall penetrations • Upgrading wall insulation • Replacing windows • Adding window film covering • Repairing windows • Sealing windows	**IAQ/Health Risks** • Asbestos-containing material, lead paint, PCBs or mold may be disturbed. • Installing spray-polyurethane foam may generate indoor contaminants. • Sealing the building envelope may increase levels of indoor contaminants, including radon, combustion by-products, moisture and mold, and VOCs. Adequate ventilation must be provided to dilute and remove indoor pollutants. Radon mitigation systems may become necessary. **Opportunities** • Control moisture and condensation potential on surfaces; install moisture-resistant insulation; and ensure proper exterior drainage and water management (e.g., include header and panned windowsill flashing during window replacement). • Seal unwanted openings and leaks in the building envelope to reduce infiltration and conditions conducive to pest entry.	1.0 Project Planning/Integrated Design 2.0 Commissioning 3.0 Moisture Control and Mold 4.0 Asbestos 5.0 Lead 6.0 PCBs 7.0 Radon 8.0 Belowground Vapor-Forming Contaminants 9.0 Vehicle Exhaust 11.0 Pests 13.0 Building Products/Materials Emissions 14.0 Vented Combustion Appliances 15.0 Unvented Combustion Appliances 19.0 Outdoor Air Ventilation 20.0 Exhaust Ventilation 21.0 Building Safety for Children and Other Occupants 22.0 Protecting IAQ During Construction 23.0 Jobsite Safety
Concrete Floor Sealing • Repairing and sealing floor penetrations • Sealing cracks and joints in floors • Applying floor sealer/paint	**IAQ/Health Risks** • Asbestos-containing material, lead paint, PCBs or mold may be disturbed. • Sealing the building envelope may increase levels of indoor contaminants, including radon, combustion by-products, moisture and mold, and VOCs. Adequate ventilation must be provided to dilute and remove indoor pollutants. **Opportunities** • Understand and appropriately manage moisture emission rates and select sealants/adhesives with low-VOC or no-VOC content/emissions. • Reduce infiltration and conditions conducive to pest entry. • Seal cracks and joints in floors, which may be an integral part of a radon mitigation system.	1.0 Project Planning/Integrated Design 3.0 Moisture Control and Mold 4.0 Asbestos 5.0 Lead 6.0 PCBs 7.0 Radon 8.0 Belowground Vapor-Forming Contaminants 9.0 Vehicle Exhaust 11.0 Pests 13.0 Building Products/Materials Emissions 14.0 Vented Combustion Appliances 19.0 Outdoor Air Ventilation 21.0 Building Safety for Children and Other Occupants 22.0 Protecting IAQ During Construction 23.0 Jobsite Safety

Table 1: Examples of School Energy Efficiency and Upgrade Projects (continued)

Examples of Projects With Energy Savings Plus Health Objectives	Examples of IAQ/Health Risks and Opportunities	Potentially Applicable Priority Issues
Moisture Barrier for Ground-level Slabs, Basement and Crawlspace Floors • Adding new moisture barriers • Modifying or repairing existing moisture barriers	**IAQ/Health Risks** • Asbestos-containing material, lead paint, PCBs or mold may be disturbed. • Uncovered dirt floor may contribute to excessive moisture migration into the building. • Installing carpet or floor tile over concrete floor that has a persistent condensation or water pooling problem will likely lead to mold growth. • An existing moisture barrier may also be an integral part of a radon mitigation system or other belowground contaminant mitigation measures and should not be disturbed. • Uncovered dirt floors may introduce pest populations and will promote rodent habitats. **Opportunities** • Provide sealed moisture barrier over dirt foundation floors. • Provide moisture barrier beneath concrete slabs. • Select sealants/adhesives with low-VOC or no-VOC content/emissions. • Select exposed poly films with proper flame and smoke ratings. • Incorporate other radon mitigation and belowground contaminant mitigation measures as needed.	1.0 Project Planning/Integrated Design 3.0 Moisture Control and Mold 4.0 Asbestos 5.0 Lead 6.0 PCBs 7.0 Radon 8.0 Belowground Vapor-Forming Contaminants 9.0 Vehicle Exhaust 11.0 Pests 13.0 Building Products/Materials Emissions 14.0 Vented Combustion Appliances 19.0 Outdoor Air Ventilation 21.0 Building Safety for Children and Other Occupants 22.0 Protecting IAQ During Construction 23.0 Jobsite Safety

Table 1: Examples of School Energy Efficiency and Upgrade Projects (continued)

Examples of Projects With Energy Savings Plus Health Objectives	Examples of IAQ/Health Risks and Opportunities	Potentially Applicable Priority Issues
HEATING, VENTILATION AND AIR CONDITIONING (HVAC) SYSTEMS		
Ducts, Fan Coils and Unit Ventilators • Adding or replacing ducts • Sealing and insulating air ducts • Altering or cleaning fan coil and unit ventilators	**IAQ/Health Risks** • Asbestos-containing material, lead paint, mold or other debris may be disturbed during duct installation, sealing or replacement. • Improper condensate drainage can present an opportunity for *Legionella*, bacterial or mold growth in units with cooling coils. • Humid climates may require additional dehumidification when the outdoor air supply is increased. • Ductwork that is not properly sealed and insulated can lead to condensation problems if it passes through unconditioned spaces. • Improper modifications to HVAC systems can cause unbalanced flows and pressures that can lead to increased intrusion of moisture, radon and other belowground contaminants. • Excessive moisture promotes pest infestation. • HVAC components may be contaminated with PCBs if PCBs have migrated via indoor air from caulk and/or lighting ballasts that contain PCBs. • Noisy ventilation systems, particularly unit ventilators, may be turned off by staff if they interfere with learning, which will negatively affect ventilation. **Opportunities** • Contain and do not disturb areas of significant mold contamination until these areas can be remediated. • Reduce entry of airborne contaminants into the building; maintain interior humidity levels. • Select low-VOC and formaldehyde-free products. • Provide sealed and energy-efficient ducts. • Provide proper ventilation; properly balanced HVAC systems can maintain positive pressurization indoors to reduce intrusion of moist air into the building envelope and interior zones and belowground contaminants and radon into the building.	1.0 Project Planning/Integrated Design 2.0 Commissioning 3.0 Moisture Control and Mold 4.0 Asbestos 5.0 Lead 6.0 PCBs 7.0 Radon 8.0 Belowground Vapor-Forming Contaminants 9.0 Vehicle Exhaust 10.0 Local and Regional Ambient Air Quality 11.0 Pests 13.0 Building Products/Materials Emissions 14.0 Vented Combustion Appliances 15.0 Unvented Combustion Appliances 16.0 Ozone From Indoor Sources 18.0 HVAC Equipment 19.0 Outdoor Air Ventilation 20.0 Exhaust Ventilation 21.0 Building Safety for Children and Other Occupants 22.0 Protecting IAQ During Construction 23.0 Jobsite Safety

Table 1: Examples of School Energy Efficiency and Upgrade Projects (continued)

Examples of Projects With Energy Savings Plus Health Objectives	Examples of IAQ/Health Risks and Opportunities	Potentially Applicable Priority Issues
Outdoor Air Ventilation (upgrades or modifications) • Outdoor air economizers and controls • Dedicated outdoor air systems • Filtration of outdoor ventilation air and make-up air • Local exhaust for indoor areas with strong sources of pollutants • Demand-controlled ventilation for intermittently occupied areas • Additional dehumidification, as needed for humid climates	**IAQ/Health Risks** • Asbestos-containing material or lead paint may be disturbed during wall, roof or ceiling penetrations. • Some locations may have strong sources of outdoor air pollution and require special designs. • Inappropriate use of airside economizers can lead to cool and clammy conditions and condensation on cold surfaces. • Humid climates may require additional dehumidification when the outdoor air supply is increased. • Excessive moisture promotes pest infestation. • Smoking near outdoor air ventilation intakes can increase indoor exposure to environmental tobacco smoke. • In many parts of the United States, gross overventilation of spaces may lead to extremely dry indoor conditions during the heating season and moisture issues during the cooling season, in addition to wasting energy. • Noisy ventilation systems, particularly unit ventilators, may be turned off by staff if they interfere with learning, which will negatively affect ventilation. • Outdoor air ventilation may be an integral part of a radon mitigation strategy. **Opportunities** • Ensure that outdoor air controls are working properly, while controlling for moisture. • Use suitable economizer controls. • Ensure the proper location of outdoor air intakes. • Provide outdoor air treatment (e.g., filtration and air cleaning) in areas where National Ambient Air Quality Standards for particulate matter or ozone are exceeded. • Ensure that all occupied spaces are provided with enough outdoor air and enough total air circulation. • Ensure that filter status pressure sensors and switches are calibrated regularly. • Plan for ongoing commissioning of systems that provide exhaust and supply ventilation to the school.	1.0 Project Planning/Integrated Design 2.0 Commissioning 3.0 Moisture Control and Mold 4.0 Asbestos 5.0 Lead 7.0 Radon 8.0 Belowground Vapor-Forming Contaminants 9.0 Vehicle Exhaust 10. Local and Regional Ambient Air Quality 11.0 Pests 13.0 Building Products/Materials Emissions 14.0 Vented Combustion Appliances 15.0 Unvented Combustion Appliances 16.0 Ozone From Indoor Sources 17.0 Environmental Tobacco Smoke 18.0 HVAC Equipment 19.0 Outdoor Air Ventilation 20.0 Exhaust Ventilation 21.0 Building Safety for Children and Other Occupants 22.0 Protecting IAQ During Construction 23.0 Jobsite Safety

Table 1: Examples of School Energy Efficiency and Upgrade Projects (continued)

Examples of Projects With Energy Savings Plus Health Objectives	Examples of IAQ/Health Risks and Opportunities	Potentially Applicable Priority Issues
Heating and Cooling Systems • Boiler replacement. • Steam trap replacement or maintenance • Pipe modifications: Converting from one-pipe to two-pipe steam systems OR Converting from two-pipe to four-pipe heating and cooling systems • System modifications: Converting from steam to hot-water systems • Control valves: Maintenance and additions • Combustion equipment replacement • Air conditioning system replacement	**IAQ/Health Risks** • Asbestos-containing material, lead paint or mold may be disturbed during system or component replacement. • Improperly vented combustion gases and occupant exposure to carbon monoxide are potential risks. • Moisture or mold may be present when the HVAC system is turned off for extended periods of time. • Poor humidity control during cooling system operation can result in mold growth and present opportunities for pest infestations. • Inappropriate use of chilled water reset or airside economizers can lead to cool and clammy conditions and condensation on cold surfaces. • Indoor air can become too dry for occupant comfort and health during the heating season, particularly in northern and high-altitude locations. • Inadequate humidifier maintenance can lead to microbiological problems. • HVAC components may be contaminated with PCBs if PCBs have migrated via indoor air from caulk and/or lighting ballasts that contain PCBs. **Opportunities** • Properly vent combustion gases and ensure that mechanical rooms with combustion equipment have adequate make-up air and ventilation. • Install and maintain carbon monoxide detection and warning equipment. • Ensure that steam traps, combustion equipment and boilers are installed correctly and that make-up air registers are not blocked. • Ensure that air conditioning systems are properly sized and controlled to avoid humidity and moisture issues, particularly under part-load conditions, and properly sized for both cooling and dehumidification. • Ensure that well-maintained humidification equipment and controls are in place to promote occupant comfort and health during the heating season, as needed.	1.0 Project Planning/Integrated Design 2.0 Commissioning 3.0 Moisture Control and Mold 4.0 Asbestos 5.0 Lead 6.0 PCBs 7.0 Radon 8.0 Belowground Vapor-Forming Contaminants 9.0 Vehicle Exhaust 10.0 Local and Regional Ambient Air Quality 11.0 Pests 13.0 Building Products/Materials Emissions 14.0 Vented Combustion Appliances 15.0 Unvented Combustion Appliances 16.0 Ozone From Indoor Sources 18.0 HVAC Equipment 19.0 Outdoor Air Ventilation 20.0 Exhaust Ventilation 21.0 Building Safety for Children and Other Occupants 22.0 Protecting IAQ During Construction 23.0 Jobsite Safety

Table 1: Examples of School Energy Efficiency and Upgrade Projects (continued)

Examples of Projects With Energy Savings Plus Health Objectives	Examples of IAQ/Health Risks and Opportunities	Potentially Applicable Priority Issues
HVAC Controls to Monitor/ Maintain IAQ (upgrades or modifications) • Temperature and humidity controls: Installation, replacement and/or calibration • Direct digital control systems with sensor-based control points for humidity, temperature, carbon dioxide or pressure • Building automation system that controls outdoor air and exhaust flow rates • Air filtration pressure sensors • Occupancy sensors	**IAQ/Health Risks** • Asbestos-containing material or lead paint may be disturbed during wall or ceiling penetrations. • Mercury from removal of old mercury bulb thermostats may present a risk. • Sensors that are not regularly calibrated may lead to IAQ problems. • Poor humidity control during cooling system operation can result in mold growth and present opportunities for pest infestations. • Inappropriate use of chilled water reset or airside economizers can lead to cool and clammy conditions and condensation on cold surfaces. • Indoor air can become too dry for occupant comfort and health during the heating season, particularly in northern and high-altitude locations. • Inadequate operation and maintenance of humidifier controls can lead to microbiological problems. • Improper HVAC controls can cause unbalanced flows and pressures that can lead to increased intrusion of moisture, radon and other belowground contaminants. • Improperly vented combustion gases; occupant exposure to carbon monoxide. **Opportunities** • Control moisture to avoid mold growth and pest infestations, and optimize occupant comfort. • Ensure that well-maintained humidification equipment and controls are in place to promote occupant comfort and health during the heating season, as needed. • Monitor and maintain outdoor airflow rates. • Install and maintain carbon monoxide detection and warning equipment. • Properly dispose of mercury-containing thermostats.	1.0 Project Planning/Integrated Design 2.0 Commissioning 3.0 Moisture Control and Mold 4.0 Asbestos 5.0 Lead 7.0 Radon 8.0 Belowground Vapor-Forming Contaminants 9.0 Vehicle Exhaust 10.0 Local and Regional Ambient Air Quality 11.0 Pests 13.0 Building Products/Materials Emissions 14.0 Vented Combustion Appliances 15.0 Unvented Combustion Appliances 16.0 Ozone From Indoor Sources 18.0 HVAC Equipment 19.0 Outdoor Air Ventilation 20.0 Exhaust Ventilation 21.0 Building Safety for Children and Other Occupants 22.0 Protecting IAQ During Construction 23.0 Jobsite Safety

Table 1: Examples of School Energy Efficiency and Upgrade Projects (continued)

Examples of Projects With Energy Savings Plus Health Objectives	Examples of IAQ/Health Risks and Opportunities	Potentially Applicable Priority Issues
Hydronic Systems (upgrades or modifications) • Chilled water system optimization • Pipe insulation upgrades (chilled water, hot water, steam piping) • Hydronic or steam piping system changes • Cooling towers upgrades	**IAQ/Health Risks** • Asbestos-containing material, lead paint or mold may be disturbed during system or component replacement. • Moisture accumulation on cold surfaces can lead to mold growth and pest infestations. • *Legionella* bacteria can grow in stagnant water, including hot water tanks. • Poor maintenance of cooling tower will allow *Legionella* bacteria to grow, causing potential risk to maintenance personnel and occupants. **Opportunities** • Control moisture to prevent mold growth and pest infestations and optimize occupant comfort. • Manage building water systems and cooling towers to minimize bacteria growth and prevent legionellosis.	1.0 Project Planning/Integrated Design 2.0 Commissioning 3.0 Moisture Control and Mold 4.0 Asbestos 5.0 Lead 7.0 Radon 8.0 Belowground Vapor-Forming Contaminants 9.0 Vehicle Exhaust 13.0 Building Products/Materials Emissions 14.0 Vented Combustion Appliances 15.0 Unvented Combustion Appliances 16.0 Ozone From Indoor Sources 18.0 HVAC Equipment 19.0 Outdoor Air Ventilation 20.0 Exhaust Ventilation 21.0 Building Safety for Children and Other Occupants 22.0 Protecting IAQ During Construction 23.0 Jobsite Safety
MATERIALS SELECTION AND REPLACEMENT		
Adhesives and Sealants • Application of materials used during energy upgrades for air sealing • Application of materials used for adhering and fastening components	**IAQ/Health Risks** • Asbestos-containing material, lead paint or PCBs may be disturbed when removing previously installed adhesives or sealants. • Weatherization and air sealing can reduce air exchange rates and result in elevated levels of contaminants indoors if there is inadequate ventilation. **Opportunities** • Always select sealants and adhesives for indoor use with low-VOC or no-VOC content/emissions. • Select outdoor sealants for long life to keep out water and, when possible, with low-VOC or no-VOC content/emissions. • Ensure adequate outdoor air ventilation after weatherization and air sealing.	1.0 Project Planning/Integrated Design 4.0 Asbestos 5.0 Lead 6.0 PCBs 13.0 Building Products/Materials Emissions 21.0 Building Safety for Children and Other Occupants 22.0 Protecting IAQ During Construction 23.0 Jobsite Safety

Table 1: Examples of School Energy Efficiency and Upgrade Projects (continued)

Examples of Projects With Energy Savings Plus Health Objectives	Examples of IAQ/Health Risks and Opportunities	Potentially Applicable Priority Issues
Carpet and Flooring • Replacing existing carpet • Installing new carpet over uncarpeted areas • Replacing or repairing existing floor tiles • Installing new flooring over existing floor surfaces	**IAQ/Health Risks** • Asbestos-containing material (many floor tiles in older buildings, including schools, were made of asbestos), lead paint, mold or large quantities of dust may be disturbed. • Carpet and flooring may be contaminated with PCBs if PCBs have migrated via indoor air from caulk and/or lighting ballasts that contain PCBs. **Opportunities** • Isolate the work area to reduce dust migration caused by carpet and flooring removal. • Select low-VOC materials, including carpets, resilient flooring, adhesives and sealants.	1.0 Project Planning/Integrated Design 3.0 Moisture Control and Mold 4.0 Asbestos 5.0 Lead 6.0 PCBs 12.0 Tracked-In Pollutants 13.0 Building Products/Materials Emissions 21.0 Building Safety for Children and Other Occupants 22.0 Protecting IAQ During Construction 23.0 Jobsite Safety
Painting • Removing old deteriorated paint (scraping and sanding) • Repainting existing surfaces • Painting new surfaces	**IAQ/Health Risks** • Asbestos-containing material, lead paint or PCBs may be disturbed. • Indoor surfaces may be contaminated with PCBs if PCBs have migrated via indoor air from caulk and/or lighting ballasts that contain PCBs. **Opportunities** • Select paint with low-VOC or no-VOC content/emissions and do not conduct dry sanding without rigorous containment.	1.0 Project Planning/Integrated Design 4.0 Asbestos 5.0 Lead 6.0 PCBs 13.0 Building Products/Materials Emissions 21.0 Building Safety for Children and Other Occupants 22.0 Protecting IAQ During Construction 23.0 Jobsite Safety
Suspended Ceilings • Repairing or replacing existing ceiling tiles • Installing new ceilings	**IAQ/Health Risks** • Asbestos-containing material (including vermiculite insulation), fiberglass, mineral wool or other insulation materials may be disturbed. • Ceiling tiles may be contaminated with lead paint or lead paint particles. • Removal of ceiling tiles may expose pest infestations. • Ceiling tiles may have water damage and/or mold growth. • Ceiling materials may be contaminated with PCBs if PCBs have migrated from older, leaking lighting ballasts that contain PCBs. **Opportunities** • Select low-emission materials, such as formaldehyde-free ceiling tiles.	1.0 Project Planning/Integrated Design 3.0 Moisture Control and Mold 4.0 Asbestos 5.0 Lead 6.0 PCBs 9.0 Vehicle Exhaust 11.0 Pests 13.0 Building Products/Materials Emissions 21.0 Building Safety for Children and Other Occupants 22.0 Protecting IAQ During Construction 23.0 Jobsite Safety

Table 1: Examples of School Energy Efficiency and Upgrade Projects (continued)

Examples of Projects With Energy Savings Plus Health Objectives	Examples of IAQ/Health Risks and Opportunities	Potentially Applicable Priority Issues
OPERATION AND MAINTENANCE		
Systems Operation and Maintenance • Check control systems and devices for evidence of improper operation on a regular schedule (e.g., semiannually) and take corrective actions • Calibrate and periodically recalibrate sensors (e.g., temperature, humidity, carbon dioxide) • Perform cooling unit drain pan maintenance • Replace filters • Clean supply diffusers, return registers and outside air intakes • Keep unit ventilators and other duct openings clear of obstructions (e.g., books, papers, other items) • Perform regular system operational checks • Calibrate occupancy sensors • Calibrate daylight sensors	**IAQ/Health Risks** • Asbestos-containing material, lead paint, PCBs or mold may be disturbed. • Deferred maintenance can lead to system degradation and IAQ problems. • Improperly maintained and uncalibrated sensors can lead to poor system performance and IAQ problems. • Poor air filtration and maintenance can lead to clogged coils and a need for expensive cleaning that can be avoided with proper maintenance. • Inadequate drain pan design or maintenance can lead to severe microbial contamination of HVAC systems. • Inadequately maintained combustion equipment can result in improperly vented combustion gases and occupant exposure to carbon monoxide. **Opportunities** • Ensure the proper operation and venting of combustion appliances. • Install and maintain carbon monoxide detection and warning equipment. • Control for moisture by maintaining humidity levels. • Ensure that particle removal filtration systems are operating properly. • Repair or adjust drain pans to drain completely. • Ensure that occupancy sensors are operating properly. • Implement a scheduled inspection and calibration/recalibration program (e.g., semiannually) for measurement sensors, paying special attention to the systems that are intended to supply adequate ventilation to the school. • During commissioning, train HVAC system operators to recognize when sensors are indicating problems with HVAC system function that may lead to IAQ problems. • Maintain comfortable indoor temperatures to facilitate learning.	1.0 Project Planning/Integrated Design 2.0 Commissioning 3.0 Moisture Control and Mold 4.0 Asbestos 5.0 Lead 7.0 Radon 8.0 Belowground Vapor-Forming Contaminants 9.0 Vehicle Exhaust 10.0 Local and Regional Ambient Air Quality 11.0 Pests 13.0 Building Products/Materials Emissions 14.0 Vented Combustion Appliances 15.0 Unvented Combustion Appliances 16.0 Ozone From Indoor Sources 18.0 HVAC Equipment 19.0 Outdoor Air Ventilation 20.0 Exhaust Ventilation 21.0 Building Safety for Children and Other Occupants 22.0 Protecting IAQ During Construction 23.0 Jobsite Safety

Table 1: Examples of School Energy Efficiency and Upgrade Projects (continued)

Examples of Projects With Energy Savings Plus Health Objectives	Examples of IAQ/Health Risks and Opportunities	Potentially Applicable Priority Issues
Building Operations and Maintenance • Deep extraction steam or hot water carpet cleaning • Pest control • Custodial operations	**IAQ/Health Risks** • Asbestos-containing material, lead paint, PCBs or mold may be disturbed. • Cleaning chemicals and pesticides may aggravate allergies and asthma. • Mold and moisture problems may occur if carpets do not dry quickly after spills or carpet cleaning. • Smoking near outdoor air ventilation intakes can increase indoor exposure to environmental tobacco smoke. • Vehicle idling near outdoor air intakes can increase indoor exposure to vehicle exhaust contaminants. **Opportunities** • Minimize chemical exposure to occupants and staff by using the least toxic materials. • Reduce cleaning product use through better use of cleaning equipment and cleaning process improvements. • Minimize exposure to pesticides through integrated pest management tactics. • Always plan for thorough drying of carpets if steam or wet methods are used, especially during humid weather. • Provide walk-off mats to reduce track-in of pollutants. • Ensure that the school has a policy on tobacco use that prohibits tobacco use on school property and is consistent with local, state and federal laws. • Ensure that the school has a vehicle anti-idling policy. • Periodically retest areas of the school that have been mitigated for radon.	1.0 Project Planning/Integrated Design 2.0 Commissioning 3.0 Moisture Control and Mold 4.0 Asbestos 5.0 Lead 6.0 PCBs 7.0 Radon 8.0 Belowground Vapor-Forming Contaminants 9.0 Vehicle Exhaust 11.0 Pests 12.0 Tracked-In Pollutants 13.0 Building Products/Materials Emissions 14.0 Vented Combustion Appliances 15.0 Unvented Combustion Appliances 16.0 Ozone From Indoor Sources 17.0 Environmental Tobacco Smoke 18.0 HVAC Equipment 21.0 Building Safety for Children and Other Occupants 22.0 Protecting IAQ During Construction 23.0 Jobsite Safety

Table 1: Examples of School Energy Efficiency and Upgrade Projects (continued)

Examples of Projects With Energy Savings Plus Health Objectives	Examples of IAQ/Health Risks and Opportunities	Potentially Applicable Priority Issues
School Building Summer Schedule • Reduce energy consumption during extended periods of non-use • Monitor indoor conditions (temperature, relative humidity and, if possible, dew point) and adjust HVAC systems to maintain indoor conditions that prevent moisture problems and mold growth • Consider incorporating an alarm to detect and alert for an excessive indoor relative humidity or dew point condition	**IAQ/Health Risks** • Indoor moisture and mold problems can be caused by lack of cooling system operation and dehumidification and by indoor moisture-generating activities, such as carpet cleaning and painting. • Drain traps, including floor drains, may dry out if not used for an extended period. **Opportunities** • Control moisture by monitoring temperature, relative humidity and condensation and specifying HVAC operation to maintain indoor conditions that prevent moisture/mold problems. • Use high-efficiency commercial dehumidifiers when needed if air conditioning systems are cycled off as sensible cooling loads decrease. • Use high-efficiency commercial dehumidifiers during and after "wet" activities, such as carpet cleaning, wall cleaning and painting. • If air conditioning is provided during the shutdown period, continue filter maintenance during the summer if warranted. • Consider changing filters after the air conditioning season or the humid weather season has ended. • Ensure that drain traps do not dry out, either through scheduled maintenance or installation of automatic drain trap primers.	1.0 Project Planning/Integrated Design 2.0 Commissioning 3.0 Moisture Control and Mold 8.0 Belowground Vapor-Forming Contaminants 11.0 Pests 13.0 Building Products/Materials Emissions 15.0 Unvented Combustion Appliances 21.0 Building Safety for Children and Other Occupants 22.0 Protecting IAQ During Construction 23.0 Jobsite Safety

The Business Case for Integrating Energy Efficiency and IAQ

In the coming decades, school districts are likely to make substantial investments in renovating existing school buildings and performing equipment upgrades (also called retrofits). Because U.S. schools spend more than $7.5 billion annually on energy to maintain functioning classrooms and buildings (EPA ENERGY STAR®, 2008), many of the future improvements will aim to reduce energy use, while providing adequate ventilation and saving money. When-ever new school design and construction, major renovations and/or targeted building retrofits occur, or whenever regular operations and maintenance practices are improved, school officials have a well-timed opportunity to simultaneously protect IAQ, integrate healthy practices and save money. Through up-front planning, coordination and open communication among all stakeholders, schools can make this integration work successfully.

Studies have demonstrated that increased classroom ventilation rates are associated with improvements in student health and performance. A European study showed that a doubling of the ventilation rate from about 7.5 cubic feet per minute per person (cfm/person) to 15 cfm/person improved speed of academic performance by about 8 percent (Wargocki & Wyon, 2006). A U.S. study in fifth-grade classrooms from 100 schools used student performance in standard academic tests as the measure of performance and estimated that there was nearly a 3-percent increase in the proportion of students passing standardized math and reading tests for each 2 cfm/person increase in ventilation rate across the range of 2 to 15 cfm/person (Haverinen-Shaugnessy et al., 2011). A recent study also demonstrated that for each 2.1 cfm/person increase in ventilation rate, on average, the illness absence of students decreased by 1.6 percent (Mendell et al., 2013). In some school districts, income from government sources is linked to days of student attendance; thus, increased ventilation rates may increase school district income. Indoor temperature also can affect occupant performance. For example, one study showed that the average speed of completing academic work, based on monitoring of performance of eight simulated school work tasks, decreased by approximately 1 percent per each 1 °F as temperatures increased from 68 °F to 77 °F (Wargocki & Wyon, 2006). A detailed discussion of how IAQ parameters can affect student health and academic performance, with supporting references, can also be located at the IAQ Scientific Findings Resource Bank website, hosted by the Lawrence Berkeley National Laboratory.

Well-conceived and coordinated school energy and IAQ management programs can save money. A report, *Greening America's Schools: Costs and Benefits,* reviewed 30 green schools and concluded that green schools cost on average 2 percent more than conventional schools, but the financial benefits derived are about 20 times greater than the additional costs (Kats, 2006). "Green" schools were defined as new schools based on either the U.S. Green Building Council's Leadership in Energy and Environmental Design program, the Massachusetts Collaborative for High Performance Schools, or the Washington State Sustainable School Protocol for High Performance Facilities. By understanding the relationship between typical energy management activities and IAQ, and by following the guidance recommended in this Energy Saving Plus Health Guide, schools can potentially realize substantial improvements in IAQ and cost savings.

Cost savings from energy efficiency and IAQ integration can be significant and easy to achieve. For example, the Blue Valley School District in Overland Park, Kansas, identified a leader for its IAQ team and began with "quick wins" that would improve IAQ with minimal effort and cost. Building on these small successes, the district moved on to larger and broader goals, making strategic connections between energy efficiency and IAQ goals to combine resources and achieve greater success. A new mechanical system in one of its schools resulted in not only increased outdoor air ventilation but also cost savings of $23,000 annually from the reduction in energy use. Blue Valley capitalizes on energy savings and directs money into the operat-

> By understanding the relationship between typical energy management activities and IAQ, and by following the guidance recommended in this Energy Saving Plus Health Guide, schools can potentially realize substantial improvements in IAQ and cost savings.

ing budget, which provides resources for more energy efficiency and IAQ improvements. The district tracks outcomes of bond-financed facility improvements and demonstrates costs savings that then are applied to IAQ management activities. This is an effective strategy when the district does not have the budget to make the initial investment in improvements and ultimately helps provide more resources for additional projects. In 2006, Blue Valley was the first school district in the nation to receive the *IAQ Tools for Schools* National Model of Sustained Excellence Award from EPA.

Similarly, in Colorado Springs School District 11, the integration of energy efficiency and IAQ had remarkable benefits. The district's energy management program—built on the commitment of the superintendent, board of education, and a full-time coordinator—has resulted in an estimated annual energy savings of more than $928,000 and significant IAQ improvements. IAQ goals have been accomplished through energy-efficient design, proper maintenance and commissioning of HVAC equipment, and the use of performance-based contracting for improvements in existing schools. Colorado Springs School District 11 previously won the ENERGY STAR® Partner of the Year Award in 2005.

There are measurable costs for not promoting healthy school environments. The costs imposed by environmentally attributable diseases—such as asthma—on children, families and schools are immense (Landrigan et al., 2002). According to the Centers for Disease Control and Prevention (CDC), the annual economic cost of asthma, including direct medical costs from hospital stays and indirect costs (e.g., lost school and work days), amounts to more than $56 billion annually (CDC, 2011). For states, a large percentage of these costs can be attributed to health care expenditures, lost school days and lost productivity (e.g., parents having to stay home to care for a sick child). Given the amount of time that children spend in school each day, high-quality school environments are critically important for ensuring that children are healthy and able to perform in the classroom (EPA State School Environmental Health Guidelines, 2012).

An Integrated Approach to Energy Efficiency and IAQ:

Case Studies of Demonstrated Results

Blue Valley School District, Kansas:

- Mechanical retrofit of a 260,000 square-foot (ft^2) building resulted in energy cost savings of 18–20 percent in the first year.

- Replacement of a heat pump in one building with a new ventilation system resulted in a 30-percent drop in energy consumption at the same time as the outdoor air ventilation rates increased.

- A districtwide environmental management system continually monitors, identifies and pinpoints potential energy and IAQ issues early, reducing the costs associated with maintenance staff diagnosing problems.

- The maintenance of modern equipment is associated with lower costs.

- There have been fewer IAQ complaints and associated repairs.

- The long-term goal is the mechanical upgrades of 100 percent of facilities to capture energy savings and improve IAQ.

For more information, see http://epa.gov/iaq/schools/casestudies/Blue_Valley.pdf.

Colorado Springs School District 11, Colorado:

- The district's energy program realizes $1.8 million in annual energy cost savings in comparison with costs before the program was established.

- $55.5 million in energy costs have been saved during the past 12 years as a result of energy efficiency and IAQ improvements.

- All new facilities built have the following qualities:

    o Low energy consumption: Energy use intensity of 25 kBtu/ft^2 per year or less.

    o Low energy use for lighting: 0.7 Watts/ft^2 or less of artificial light.

    o Bright and well-lit classrooms: Maintain 35 foot-candles in classrooms.

- Ongoing commissioning keeps energy waste, and therefore costs, down while ensuring IAQ problems are identified and remedied quickly.

- In 2012, 32 of the district's buildings were certified ENERGY STAR® buildings, with low energy costs and healthier indoor environments.

For more information, see http://www.energystar.gov/ia/business/k12_schools/ENERGY_STAR_Case_Study-Achieving_Healthy_Indoor_Environments_CG0807.pdf.

Section 2

Assessment Protocols and
Recommended Actions

Integrated Process

Introductory Note for Priority Issues 1.0 Project Planning/Integrated Design and 2.0 Commissioning

A wide range of school building upgrade projects is possible, from small-scale retrofits of components/systems to much larger and more extensive projects involving modifications to multiple building systems and major renovations to the school building. A project's planning, design and commissioning processes will depend on its magnitude and unique characteristics. It is appropriate for users of this Guide to tailor their requirements for Priority Issues 1.0 Project Planning/ Integrated Design and 2.0 Commissioning. For example, simpler projects with limited goals and funding may need a less formal design process and commissioning than larger-scale renovation projects. Project teams should be aware of the potential benefits associated with adequate project planning and commissioning to ensure that buildings and systems are designed, installed and operating as intended and in line with the schools' expectations and requirements. Assessment Protocols, Minimum Actions and Expanded Actions related to contaminants and building systems begin with Priority Issue 3.0 Moisture Control and Mold.

PRIORITY ISSUE 1.0 PROJECT PLANNING/INTEGRATED DESIGN		
ASSESSMENT PROTOCOLS (AP)	**MINIMUM ACTIONS (MA)**	**EXPANDED ACTIONS (EA)**
AP 1.1 Gather Feedback on IAQ Conditions in the School Building Gather feedback from the school's faculty and staff, including the IAQ coordinator (if one exists), the custodian and the school nurse. Determine locations in the building with IAQ concerns or complaints and gain an understanding of the current building status to inform the project team.  Conduct stakeholder meetings early in the process to further identify IAQ concerns and ensure that the project meets its stated goals. Stakeholders could include, for example, teachers, administrators, nurses, maintenance staff, community leaders, parents and/or students. Use the information gathered in this step to guide the IAQ walkthrough inspection of AP 1.2. *Notes* • *A school's IAQ coordinator could be any of several professions typically found in a school, including a teacher, administrator, nurse or maintenance personnel.* • *If data on school-specific health measures are available (e.g., asthma prevalence, absenteeism rates), they may help guide the IAQ assessment. Some states require schools to keep asthma and allergy incident reports, which also could be helpful.*	**MA 1.1 Conduct Collaborative Planning Meetings** Collaboration during renovation projects can allow project teams to solve problems creatively and with better outcomes for the building and occupants. These collaborative meetings can help to identify synergies between building systems that can significantly reduce energy consumption, promote IAQ and provide cost savings. For best results, establish cross-functional team meetings from the very beginning of project planning and continue meetings regularly through project completion. For large projects, the first team meeting often is called a Design Charrette. This is a meeting at which design professionals meet with building owners, occupants and other stakeholders to understand their goals and concerns and brainstorm ways to achieve these goals within the overall project scope. Include the school's IAQ coordinator, risk manager, maintenance staff, nurses and teaching staff in this process, as staff and other building occupants often better understand a building's IAQ issues. **MA 1.2 Formalize Project Goals** For improvement projects that include several building systems, use the results of the collaborative team meetings and/or Design Charrette to more formally document IAQ goals for the project in an Owner's Project Requirements document, as outlined in MA 2.2. Formalize project goals with IAQ considerations as early as possible in the project planning/design process to allow early consideration of alternative design concepts and avoid problems that occur when IAQ is treated as an afterthought.	This cell is intentionally blank.

 See Appendix B: Communication and Education

ASSESSMENT PROTOCOLS (AP)	MINIMUM ACTIONS (MA)	EXPANDED ACTIONS (EA)

AP 1.2 Perform an IAQ Walkthrough Inspection

Perform a building walkthrough inspection to further understand IAQ and health concerns. Review each space that will potentially be included in the project. Conduct the IAQ walkthrough inspection during normal school operating hours and occupancy conditions.

If a walkthrough energy audit is performed to determine energy conservation opportunities, include the IAQ walkthrough inspection as a concurrent, integrated process.

Talk to the energy auditors and ask if they or other professionals with knowledge of the building can assist with the IAQ assessments. Ensure that the auditor/inspector determines whether the outdoor ventilation rates are sufficient and controls are functional.

Ensure that the IAQ walkthrough inspection includes aspects of pest management to evaluate pest-specific issues (e.g., evidence of infestations, pest populations, pesticide storage). See Priority Issue 11.0 Pests for additional information.

Ensure that the IAQ walkthrough inspection also includes aspects of moisture control (see AP 3.1).

For more information about IAQ walkthrough inspections, refer to EPA's *IAQ Tools for Schools* Action Kit, which illustrates common IAQ problems found in schools. The Building Air Quality guide created by EPA and CDC may also be used as a resource for IAQ walkthrough inspections. Chapter 5 of the ENERGY STAR® *Building Upgrade Manual* provides information on examining a building and its energy-consuming equipment.

MA 1.3 Finalize the Project Team

If a full project team was not selected during AP 1.3, select the remaining team members. Refer to Appendix A to assemble the appropriate project team. Make sure that the design and construction teams include IAQ expertise and that a representative from the building operation and maintenance team is included.

MA 1.4 Hold Regular Team Meetings and Communicate With Stakeholders

 Hold regular meetings throughout design and construction to discuss progress, synergies and challenges. Include the project design and construction teams regularly in meetings, and ensure that representatives from the school are present at each meeting. Refer to the ASHRAE Indoor Air Quality Guide Section 1.1 for more information on the benefits of integrated meetings. Regularly communicate project plans and progress with stakeholders (including staff, teachers and parents), and promptly respond to concerns.

MA 1.5 Hold a Construction Kick-Off Meeting

 Before construction begins, hold a construction kick-off meeting with the design team, general contractor and site managers for each trade. Use this meeting to review the overall design goals related to IAQ and energy efficiency. Specifically discuss methods the construction team will use to meet each goal and any requirements for the construction teams to document their compliance. Continue integrated team meetings with the design team, construction team and school representative(s) regularly throughout construction to ensure that any concerns or questions are addressed quickly, and continue to provide updates to staff, teachers and parents. Ensure that the plan for protecting students and other occupants during the construction phases is adequately communicated throughout the school community and a formal process is followed for responding to complaints and concerns.

See Appendix B: Communication and Education

ASSESSMENT PROTOCOLS (AP)	MINIMUM ACTIONS (MA)	EXPANDED ACTIONS (EA)
AP 1.3 Define General Goals and Develop a Communications Plan Generally define the project scope, considering IAQ findings, energy efficiency goals and project budget. Determine whether the project will be a major renovation or addition, which will require a larger project team, or if it will be a smaller system(s) upgrade. Ensure that the project's specifications and procurement documentation (e.g., Request for Proposals) include the specific IAQ and energy efficiency requirements. Develop a communications plan to share the project's goals with occupants and other stakeholders, with a clear process for acknowledging and addressing their feedback and concerns. **AP 1.4 Select a Project Team** Based on the overall goals of the project, form a project team as outlined in Appendix A. When evaluating proposals, ensure that the project's IAQ and energy efficiency requirements are adequately addressed, and ensure architects, engineers, commissioning agents and construction teams have experience with the type of projects being considered. Ensure that proposals include specific requirements for protecting students and other occupants during the construction phases, particularly if the building is occupied during construction. Make sure that the design and construction teams include IAQ expertise. Include a representative from each group of stakeholders in the building, for example, teachers, administrators, nurses, maintenance staff, parents and students, if possible. *Note* *Including school maintenance staff on the project team helps to ensure that design goals take maintenance challenges into account and that the maintenance team understands the design objectives of any new systems. School maintenance staff often can service facilities more effectively with simpler systems that are easily accessible.*		

References for Priority Issue 1.0 Project Planning / Integrated Design:

ASHRAE Indoor Air Quality Guide, Section 1.1

ASHRAE Procedures for Commercial Building Energy Audits

ASHRAE Standard 189.1, Informative Appendix H

CDC National Institute for Occupational Safety and Health (NIOSH): Dampness and Mold Assessment Tool

EPA and CDC-NIOSH: *Building Air Quality: A Guide for Building Owners and Facility Managers*

EPA Energy Star® *Building Upgrade Manual*

EPA *IAQ Tools for Schools, IAQ Coordinator's Guide: A Guide to Implementing an IAQ Program*

EPA *IAQ Tools for Schools,* IAQ Reference Guide, Section 3 – Effective Communication

EPA *IAQ Tools for Schools,* The *Indoor Air Quality Tools for Schools* Approach: Providing a Framework for Success

EPA *IAQ Tools for Schools* Action Kit: Ventilation Checklist

EPA IAQ Tools for Schools Action Kit: Walkthrough Inspection Checklist

EPA State School Environmental Health Guidelines

National Institute of Building Sciences Whole Building Design Guide: Planning and Conducting Integrated Design (ID) Charrettes

Sheet Metal and Air Conditioning Contractors' National Association (SMACNA) IAQ Guidelines for Occupied Buildings Under Construction, Second Edition

 See Appendix B: Communication and Education

ASSESSMENT PROTOCOLS (AP)	MINIMUM ACTIONS (MA)	EXPANDED ACTIONS (EA)

AP 2.1 Review Commissioning Options

Commissioning is a quality-focused process intended to verify and document that buildings and building systems are constructed, installed, configured and performing in a manner consistent with the design intent. There are several types of commissioning:

- Commissioning for new systems, performed as part of an improvement or new construction project.

- Recommissioning, covering any previously commissioned systems and performed after an improvement project is complete.

- Retro-commissioning, covering existing systems and performed as part of an improvement project.

Examples of school building systems that have significant potential to impact IAQ, and thus should be considered during commissioning, include the building envelope, HVAC systems and associated controls, kitchen equipment, and fume hoods.

More information about commissioning is in Appendix A.

MA 2.1 Designate a Commissioning Agent

As appropriate for the project, designate or hire a Commissioning Agent early in the design process. For smaller projects, it may be appropriate to perform commissioning activities with in-house staff or consultants. Carefully select a professional with experience installing, maintaining or monitoring the types of systems to be upgraded, as someone with extensive HVAC commissioning experience may not be an expert in building envelope commissioning. Refer to the ASHRAE Indoor Air Quality Guide, Strategy 1.2, or EPA's *IAQ Design Tools for Schools*, Commissioning Guidance, for further guidance on selecting an appropriate Commissioning Agent for larger projects.

MA 2.2 Develop the Owner's Project Requirements Document

Clearly outline the IAQ and energy efficiency goals of the project by developing an Owner's Project Requirements document. This document will be used throughout the design, construction, inspection and testing phases to ensure that overall goals are met.

Use results from the following to determine the IAQ goals to be achieved by the project:

- AP 1.1 Gather Feedback on IAQ Conditions in the School Building

- AP 1.2 Perform an IAQ Walkthrough Inspection

- MA 1.1 Conduct Collaborative Planning Meetings

ASHRAE Indoor Air Quality Guide Strategy 1.2 provides further guidance on the importance of the Owner's Project Requirements document.

EA 2.1 Design for Ongoing Measurement and Verification

Design for ongoing measurement and verification of IAQ parameters by including measurement devices, such as outdoor airflow measurement devices, carbon dioxide sensors and humidity sensors. These devices can help identify IAQ problems caused by occupancy or building operation and help to quickly identify malfunctioning systems.

EA 2.2 Plan for Recommissioning

As systems age, operational guidelines may not be followed, and systems and their sequences of operation may degrade. If significant IAQ complaints arise or energy consumption suddenly increases, consider performing an audit of the building HVAC systems and hiring a Commissioning Agent to recommission any systems that are no longer calibrated properly. Refer to the ENERGY STAR® *Building Upgrade Manual*, Chapter 5.

EA 2.3 Conduct Follow-Up Operator Training

Conduct follow-up training (e.g., 6 months or 1 year after the initial training). This will reinforce operator skills and knowledge and provide an opportunity for operators to ask questions after they become familiar with the upgraded building and systems. Consider recording training sessions for future reference by operators.

MA 2.3 Develop a Basis of Design Document

A Basis of Design document should be developed by the design team to outline how the design will meet the Owner's Project Requirements. For further details on creating a Basis of Design, refer to the ASHRAE Indoor Air Quality Guide, Strategy 1.2, or the Collaborative for High Performance Schools Best Practices, Volume V: Commissioning for High Performance Schools.

MA 2.4 Develop a Commissioning Plan

The Commissioning Plan serves as a guide for the commissioning process and informs project stakeholders about commissioning activities, responsibilities and milestones. The Commissioning Plan also identifies the systems that must be commissioned and provides specifications to integrate into the project documentation.

Projects that include modifications to the HVAC system, building envelope and cooling towers and projects that include "innovative" systems (e.g., energy recovery ventilation, under-floor air distribution and displacement ventilation systems) can have an impact on IAQ and should be commissioned. Even minor system upgrades should include a quality control process, even if full commissioning is not performed.

For HVAC system commissioning, refer to ASHRAE's Guideline 0-2013, The Commissioning Process, and ASHRAE's Guideline 1.1-2007, HVAC&R Technical Requirements for the Commissioning Process.

For building envelope commissioning, refer to ASTM International's E2813-12, Standard Practice for Building Enclosure Commissioning.

If existing systems will not be upgraded in the improvement project, but were identified in the building audit as malfunctioning or not working efficiently, plan to perform retro-commissioning to correct operational deficiencies, control sequences, setpoints and other needed calibrations. For more information, see ENERGY STAR® *Building Upgrade Manual*, Chapter 5.

MA 2.5 Commission Systems

If building envelope modifications or additions are included in the improvement project, the Commissioning Agent should review the envelope design and perform onsite verification beginning during the early stages of construction. The importance of timing the commissioning activities to protect IAQ is outlined in detail in the ASHRAE Indoor Air Quality Guide, Strategy 1.2.

Two valuable aspects of commissioning are prefunctional checklists and functional performance testing that have traditionally been used for commissioning HVAC systems; these can be adapted to other building systems.

Prefunctional checklists verify the proper installation of equipment and help identify deficiencies prior to functional performance testing. These checklists are intended to supplement, not replace, any manufacturer startup checklists or documentation.

The goal of functional performance testing is to assess complete system operation and evaluate the interaction of individual components. The scope of functional performance testing includes automated controls, sequences of operation, and equipment function during various modes of operation. Testing criteria include the Owner's Project Requirements and Basis of Design documents, manufacturers' requirements, and sequences of operation.

ASSESSMENT PROTOCOLS (AP)	MINIMUM ACTIONS (MA)	EXPANDED ACTIONS (EA)
	MA 2.6 Deliver a Commissioning Report If a Commissioning Agent was hired to perform commissioning activities, a commissioning report should be provided to the facility manager, the owner or the owner's representative. The report should include an overview of the commissioning process, prefunctional checks and functional performance testing methods and detailed results, identified deficiencies, resolved issues and outstanding problems, including equipment installation and operation. The report should include dates and times for all functional checks and performance tests. The report should address the adequacy of the installed and commissioned equipment and systems in meeting the contract, Owner's Project Requirements and the Basis of Design documents. The report should be clearly written and easily understood by all members of the project team. **MA 2.7 Post-Occupancy Commissioning** Depending on the functional performance testing schedule and results, deferring certain functional performance tests (or portions thereof) to the appropriate season or weather conditions often is required. Seasonal or deferred testing can capture system performance during times when IAQ may be more acutely affected (e.g., when outdoor air ventilation rates are at design minimums during seasonal design weather conditions). Also, performing additional commissioning verification before system warranties expire may identify issues that could be resolved under warranty. **MA 2.8 Operator Training** The Commissioning Agent should provide training to the facility manager and other operations and maintenance staff on all commissioned systems, which may require a significant time investment. Operations manuals can be difficult to understand and may not provide all the information on the building's systems. The Commissioning Agent may have unique insight into system design and correct operation and should provide thorough training and documentation to facility staff at project completion. The ENERGY STAR® *Building Upgrade Manual*'s Chapter 5 on retro-commissioning outlines the type of information that should be provided during training. Document attendance for future reference and potential followup.	

References for Priority Issue 2.0 Commissioning:

ASHRAE Guideline 0-2013, The Commissioning Process
ASHRAE Guideline 1.1-2007, HVAC&R Technical Requirements for the Commissioning Process
ASHRAE Indoor Air Quality Guide, Strategy 1.2. *(See Part I Summary Guidance and Part II Detailed Guidance)*
ASTM E2813-12, Standard Practice for Building Enclosure Commissioning
Collaborative for High Performance Schools Best Practices Manual, Volume V: Commissioning of High Performance Schools
EPA *IAQ Design Tools for Schools*, Commissioning

Moisture and Mold

PRIORITY ISSUE 3.0 MOISTURE CONTROL AND MOLD		
ASSESSMENT PROTOCOLS (AP)	**MINIMUM ACTIONS (MA)**	**EXPANDED ACTIONS (EA)**

ASSESSMENT PROTOCOLS (AP)

AP 3.1 Inspect for Moisture Problems and Document Results

Inspect the interior and exterior of the building and the building's mechanical systems for evidence of moisture problems. Examples of moisture and mold problems include the following:

- Water damage or stains (e.g., on walls or ceilings)
- Foundation cracks that leak water
- Signs of seepage or wicking (e.g., efflorescence, peeling paint, delaminating materials)
- Visible mold growth
- Mold growth in duct work and plenums
- Wet or damp spots
- Musty odor
- Groundwater, surface water and rainwater intrusion
- Plumbing leaks
- Condensation or moisture damage on or around windows
- Other condensation (consider surface temperature, relative humidity and dew point temperature when evaluating the potential for condensation problems)

Document the extent and locations of the problems and the proposed repairs.

Notes

- *Building staff and occupants may be a source of information regarding past and present moisture problems.*
- *The CDC-NIOSH Dampness and Mold Assessment Tool may be a useful resource for inspecting and documenting mold and moisture problems in the school.*

MINIMUM ACTIONS (MA)

MA 3.1 Repair Moisture Problems

Repair moisture problems identified during the assessment (e.g., plumbing leaks; rain leaks, including leaks around windows and flashing; foundation leaks). It is important to correct a moisture problem at its source.

MA 3.2 Follow Professional Guidance for Conducting Mold Remediation

 Conduct any required mold remediation following professional guidance, such as EPA's Mold Remediation in Schools and Commercial Buildings and Institute of Inspection, Cleaning and Restoration Certification (IICRC) Mold Remediation Standard S520. Do not disturb mold growth without following professional guidelines.

Note

EPA does not recommend routine sampling for mold. If visible mold is present, it is important to correct the source of the moisture problem and clean up the mold. For more information on mold sampling, see EPA's Mold Remediation in Schools and Commercial Buildings.

MA 3.3 Address Standing Water Problems

Address standing water problems (e.g., surface water pooling near the foundation, water that does not drain from flat roofs and gutters). Ensure that there is adequate slope and drainage away from the building. Correct standing water problems near foundations and crawlspaces before insulating and weatherizing.

MA 3.4 Manage Rainwater

Manage rainwater in assemblies that are included in the scope of work (e.g., drainage planes and flashings). Ensure that there is adequate slope and drainage away from the building, particularly for downspouts that carry rainwater from the roof.

MA 3.5 Ensure Proper HVAC Drainage

Ensure that drain pans meet the requirements of ASHRAE Standard 62.1.

EXPANDED ACTIONS (EA)

EA 3.1 Retrofit Crawlspaces

Retrofit crawlspaces so that they are sealed, insulated, ventilated with conditioned air, properly drained and waterproofed (see EPA Moisture Control Guidance for Building Design, Construction and Maintenance, and the 2012 International Building Code, Section 1203.3.2). Install a high-capacity, energy-efficient dehumidifier in the space if the climate conditions warrant.

EA 3.2 Perform Additional Mold Remediation Activities

 Perform additional activities, beyond those required for the building upgrade project, to remediate any observed mold growth. Follow EPA or other professional guidance.

EA 3.3 Consider Ventilation Approaches That Provide Better Moisture Control

Dedicated Outdoor Air Systems (DOAS)

Consider properly designed and controlled DOAS to precondition the outdoor air and address the ventilation and dehumidification loads, with separate cooling/heating units providing temperature control in the occupied zones, as described in the ASHRAE *Humidity Control Design Guide for Commercial and Institutional Buildings*, Chapters 10 and 18.

Note

DOAS systems are typically designed to provide air at a low dew point temperature during humid season operation and can help control indoor humidity. DOAS may not entirely address low indoor humidity problems during cold, dry season operation.

Variable-Air-Volume Systems

Consider properly designed and controlled variable-air-volume systems supplying air with a low dew point temperature (e.g., 53 to 57 °F) to provide better indoor humidity control.

 See Appendix B: Communication and Education   See Appendix C: Worker Protection

ASSESSMENT PROTOCOLS (AP)	MINIMUM ACTIONS (MA)	EXPANDED ACTIONS (EA)

AP 3.2 Determine Whether Mold Remediation is Required

Determine whether the project requires mold remediation and additional moisture control measures (e.g., as determined during the moisture inspection of AP 3.1 or the IAQ walkthrough inspection of AP 1.2). Remember to identify the sources of moisture problems. Isolate and contain areas of significant mold contamination until these areas can be remediated (see MA 3.2; see EPA Mold Remediation in Schools and Commercial Buildings and IICRC Mold Remediation Standard S520 for additional information).

AP 3.3 Define Scope for Moisture Improvements

Document which moisture problems can be addressed as part of the building upgrade project and which must be repaired before certain, specific energy-conserving measures can be implemented. Work with a general contractor or other experienced building experts to make these determinations.

AP 3.4 Assess for Moisture Problems That Can Not Be Resolved Under the Project

Significant condensation or humidity problems (e.g., condensation on multiple windows, condensation in attics, or significant moisture or mold problems) may not be possible to resolve as part of an energy improvement project. In this case, do not start building upgrade projects that will reduce the school's air infiltration rate or exacerbate the moisture problems.

MA 3.6 Prevent Condensation in the Building Enclosure

Air seal the enclosure and manage air pressure relationships.

Note

Air sealing the interface between the ceiling and attic also prevents ice dams on roofs in cold, snowy climates.

Manage water vapor flow and condensing surface temperatures to avoid dew point conditions within the envelope or on other surfaces within the building whose surface temperature is expected to fall below the surrounding dew point temperature (achieved by selecting materials with the appropriate combination of thermal resistance [known as the R-value] and vapor permeability). Strictly follow all applicable building codes for vapor barrier placement.

Ensure that all piping, valves and ductwork with condensation potential are adequately insulated to reduce moisture problems. Perform a quality control review of insulation after it is installed to ensure that all surfaces are covered with airtight, vapor-impermeable insulation, including surfaces that will pass through unconditioned spaces.

Control humidity sources.

- Provide adequate ventilation and air movement, paying particular attention to damp and wet areas.
- Ensure that existing exhaust fans in potentially wet areas (e.g., locker rooms, toilet rooms, kitchens) are operating properly and vented to the outdoors. Ensure these exhaust fans are operated when needed.
- Cover earthen floors in basements and crawlspaces with sealed vapor barriers and seal sump covers.
- Ensure proper crawlspace ventilation (e.g., foundation wall vents), moisture and humidity control for the climate zone.
- Ensure proper attic ventilation, unless sealed or conditioned.

MA 3.7 Use HVAC Systems to Manage Moisture

Use HVAC systems to manage moisture inside the building.

- Ensure proper sizing when specifying new or replacement air conditioning systems. Be sure to account for all moisture loads in the calculations, including occupants, ventilation air and infiltration.
- If the relative humidity or moisture in the indoor air is high, evaluate whether the air conditioning unit has an oversized design-sensible capacity or an undersized design-latent capacity. Design-latent (dehumidification) capacity of the system should be based on design dehumidification conditions for the location (design dew point temperature and mean coincident dry bulb temperature) as described in the ASHRAE *Humidity Control Design Guide for Commercial and Institutional Buildings*, Chapter 10.
- Schools in humid climates may need dehumidification throughout the entire year. If constant-air-volume HVAC systems are used in classrooms, provide continuous humidity control based on a scheme that provides dehumidification in response to a humidistat, as described in ASHRAE *Humidity Control Design Guide for Commercial and Institutional Buildings*, Chapter 18. Alternatively, variable-air-volume systems often can provide better indoor humidity control than traditional constant-air-volume systems when the dew point at the cooling coil remains sufficiently low across a range of sensible load conditions.

Note

In humid climates, temperature control for constant-air-volume HVAC systems is unlikely to provide adequate humidity control because the ventilation air often will introduce a significant moisture load when there is a very small or negligible sensible heat load. Moisture problems occur when a thermostat controls sensible capacity without regard to latent load (relative humidity or dew point).

- Maintain indoor relative humidity below 60%, ideally between 30% and 50%, if possible, except in spaces in which occupancy and functional requirements dictate otherwise.
- Ensure the regularly scheduled maintenance of humidification equipment installed to maintain a low relative humidity limit, to avoid microbiological problems.
- Ensure proper indoor moisture control during all summer months. Schools are not necessarily vacant during summer months, as some schools have year-round activities (e.g., summer classes, summer day camps). If there is a summer shutdown program for the school building, control indoor moisture by monitoring temperature, relative humidity and condensation and specifying HVAC operation to maintain indoor conditions that prevent moisture/mold problems and maintain the indoor relative humidity within acceptable limits. Consider incorporating an alarm to alert for an excessive indoor relative humidity or dew point condition.

Note

Gymnasium floors constructed of maple typically require an indoor humidity range of 35% to 50% relative humidity to prevent damage. Although brief excursions outside this range (e.g., less than 8 hours) are typically allowed, it is an important consideration for school building summer shutdown programs.

For mechanically ventilated buildings, ensure that building meets the exfiltration requirements of ASHRAE Standard 62.1, such that the minimum outdoor air intake equals or exceeds the maximum exhaust airflow, allowing for the exceptions provided in the standard.

ASSESSMENT PROTOCOLS (AP)	MINIMUM ACTIONS (MA)	EXPANDED ACTIONS (EA)
	MA 3.8 Use Nonporous Materials in Moisture-Prone Areas Use moisture-resistant materials in areas likely to become wetted frequently, such as areas around drinking fountains. If possible, use seamless and slip-resistant materials. ***Note*** *Floor-covering manufacturers specify the maximum water vapor emission rate of concrete over which coverings such as tile and carpet can be installed. Installing a covering on concrete that exceeds the maximum emission rate may cause the covering to fail, promote mold growth, and void the manufacturer's warranty. It is recommended that the water vapor emission rate of a floor be measured before coverings are installed (even when the installation occurs long after the building was constructed).* **MA 3.9 Control Moisture During Roofing Modifications** Take precautions to control moisture during roofing modifications. For example: • Protect open roof areas from rain during construction. • Design and construct roofing systems and flashing details to ensure proper moisture barriers. • Repair roof leaks before air sealing or insulating the attic. **MA 3.10 Protect Onsite Materials From Moisture** Protect materials onsite from moisture damage. Do not install materials that show visible signs of biological growth resulting from the presence of moisture. Store and install all building products, systems and components in strict accordance with the manufacturers' printed instructions.	

References for Priority Issue 3.0 Moisture Control and Mold:

ASHRAE *Guide for Buildings in Hot and Humid Climates*
ASHRAE *Humidity Control Design Guide for Commercial and Institutional Buildings*, Chapters 10 and 18
ASHRAE Indoor Air Quality Guide, Strategies 2.1-2.5
ASHRAE Standard 62.1, Section 5
ASHRAE Standard 189.1, Section 10.3.1.5.
CDC-NIOSH: Dampness and Mold Assessment Tool
EPA *IAQ Design Tools for Schools:* Moisture Control
EPA *IAQ Tools for Schools:* IAQ Reference Guide, Appendix H: Mold and Moisture
EPA *Moisture Control Guidance for Building Design, Construction and Maintenance*
EPA Mold Remediation in Schools and Commercial Buildings
International Code Council, International Building Code, 2012 Edition
IICRC S520 Standard and Reference Guide for Professional Mold Remediation

Hazardous Materials[1]

	PRIORITY ISSUE 4.0 ASBESTOS	
ASSESSMENT PROTOCOLS (AP)	**MINIMUM ACTIONS (MA)**	**EXPANDED ACTIONS (EA)**

AP 4.1 Review School's AHERA Asbestos Management Plan
 	
Review the school's AHERA asbestos management plan to determine areas of the school that already have been identified as containing asbestos. A copy of the asbestos management plan can be obtained by contacting the school district's AHERA Designated Person. The AHERA asbestos management plan is required to be housed in the school's administrative office. If an AHERA asbestos management plan is not available, see AP 4.2.
 	
Note
 	
If a school is subject to AHERA and an asbestos management plan is not available, the school is in violation of the Toxic Substances Control Act (TSCA).
 	
AP 4.2 Inspect Building for Asbestos-Containing Material
 	
Verify that a trained and accredited asbestos building inspector has inspected the building for asbestos-containing material (ACM) or, for new construction, verify that it was determined that no asbestos was used in the building materials. For schools built without asbestos, the Asbestos-Containing Materials in Schools Rule pursuant to AHERA (40 CFR Part 763, Subpart E) does not require inspections if the building architect, project engineer or inspector signs a statement to be included in the asbestos management plan that no asbestos was used in the construction of the school building.
 	
Care must be taken around all building materials that may potentially contain asbestos. All school buildings have the potential to contain ACM. As required under the Asbestos-Containing Materials in Schools Rule pursuant to AHERA (40 CFR Part 763, Subpart E) be sure that any building material that may contain asbestos was tested for asbestos or was assumed to contain asbestos. This information will help inform occupants and construction crews of any ACM present before work is performed.
	MA 4.1 Evaluate Condition of ACM and Use Properly Trained and Accredited Personnel for Abatement or Repair
	
	Suspected ACM in good condition can be managed in place, but take caution not to disturb it. If suspected ACM is damaged (e.g., unraveling, frayed, breaking apart), immediately isolate the area(s) and consult a trained and accredited asbestos professional to determine what corrective measures should be taken. Trained and accredited asbestos professionals must separate the work area in question from occupied portions of the building using appropriate containment practices. For suspected ACM that must be disturbed as part of the project, contact an accredited and properly trained asbestos professional for abatement or repair, in accordance with federal, state or local requirements. Only a trained and accredited asbestos professional may abate, repair or remove ACM. Contact your state asbestos regulatory agency for information on how to find an accredited asbestos professional.
	
	Notes
	
	• *Most states require a license. In some states, however, a training certificate from an Asbestos Model Accreditation Plan course may suffice.*
	
	• Typically, trained and accredited professionals can repair asbestos by—
	
	  o Sealing or Encapsulating: Treating the material with a sealant that binds the asbestos fibers together or coats the material so fibers are not released. Pipe, furnace and boiler insulation often can be repaired in this manner.
	
	  o Covering or Enclosing: Placing a protective layer over or around the ACM to prevent release of fibers. Exposed insulated piping may be covered with a protective wrap or jacket.
	
	  o Removing: Removing ACM may be advantageous when remodeling or making major changes to a building that will disturb ACM or if ACM is damaged extensively and cannot be otherwise repaired (by covering, enclosing, sealing or encapsulating).
		This cell is intentionally blank.

1. For the purposes of this Guide, "hazardous materials" refers to materials frequently found in older, existing buildings—such as asbestos, lead and PCBs—which are potentially harmful to human health and/or the environment and must be removed and disposed of by licensed professionals.

 See Appendix B: Communication and Education   See Appendix C: Worker Protection

ASSESSMENT PROTOCOLS (AP)	MINIMUM ACTIONS (MA)	EXPANDED ACTIONS (EA)

AP 4.2 Inspect Building for Asbestos-Containing Material (continued)

Persons who assess ACM must be specifically trained under the Asbestos Model Accreditation Plan, in addition to those who inspect and perform response actions. Refer to the EPA *Asbestos: School Buildings* Web page for a discussion of the AHERA regulatory requirements.

If ACM is present in the school building and there is not an asbestos management plan for the school, prepare an asbestos management plan to prevent or reduce asbestos hazards.

Note

It is a significant violation of TSCA if an asbestos management plan was not prepared for the school building prior to occupancy.

Contact a trained and accredited asbestos professional to perform the asbestos inspection and prepare the asbestos management plan. For schools, the asbestos management plan shall satisfy the requirements under the implementing rules of AHERA, as published in 40 CFR, Part 763, Subpart E.

Note

Possible sources of asbestos include the following:

- *Insulation in attics and attic-like spaces (e.g., vermiculite)*
- *Wall insulation (e.g., vermiculite, insulation blocks)*
- *Hot water and steam pipes coated with asbestos material or covered with an asbestos blanket or tape*
- *Oil and coal furnaces and door gaskets with asbestos insulation*
- *Vinyl flooring (including 9"by-9" or 12"-by-12" floor tiles, vinyl sheet flooring, and the mastics and other adhesives used to secure the flooring)*
- *Cement sheet, millboard and paper used as insulation around furnaces and wood- or coal-burning appliances*
- *Soundproofing or decorative surface materials sprayed on walls or ceilings, including popcorn ceilings*
- *Patching, joint compounds, and textured paints on walls and ceilings*
- *Roofing, shingles and siding (including cement or adhesives)*
- *Transite (cement and asbestos) combustion vent or transite flue*
- *Plaster that is old enough to potentially contain asbestos*
- *Heat-resistant fabrics*

MA 4.2 Precautions for Working Around ACM

When working around ACM, do not—

- Dust, sweep or vacuum ACM debris.
- Saw, sand, scrape or drill holes in the material.
- Use abrasive pads or brushes to strip materials.

MA 4.3 Ensure Insulation Is Asbestos-Free Before Disturbing

Do not remove or disturb insulation that appears to be vermiculite (e.g., attic or wall insulation). The EPA Asbestos website provides information on vermiculate insulation and how to identify it. Since confirming whether vermiculite contains asbestos by testing is unreliable, EPA recommends assuming it contains asbestos and managing accordingly. Specifically, EPA recommends that building owners take the following precautions:

- Leave vermiculite insulation undisturbed in attic or walls.
- Do not store boxes or other items in the attic if it contains vermiculite insulation.
- Hire a professional asbestos contractor if there are plans to remodel or conduct renovations that would disturb the vermiculite in the attic or walls to make sure that the material is safely handled and/or removed.

MA 4.4 Conduct Asbestos Abatement Before Blower Door Testing

Any asbestos abatement or repair work should be completed by properly trained and accredited asbestos professionals prior to blower door testing. Exercise appropriate caution when conducting blower door testing where friable asbestos or vermiculite attic insulation is present to avoid drawing asbestos fibers into occupied spaces (e.g., positively pressurized blower door testing).

ASSESSMENT PROTOCOLS (AP)	MINIMUM ACTIONS (MA)	EXPANDED ACTIONS (EA)
 If unsure whether material contains asbestos, contact a qualified asbestos professional to assess the material.	**MA 4.5 Asbestos Clearance Air Monitoring** Following an asbestos response action in the school (asbestos abatement corrective action) pursuant to 40 CFR Part 763.90, asbestos air testing (so called "clearance" testing) must be performed to ensure that the response action was properly conducted. Contact your state asbestos regulatory agency for information on how to find a trained and accredited asbestos professional to perform this work. **Notes:**  *Appropriate identification of ACM is necessary to ensure the continued safety of the occupants and the safety of workers, who may not be aware of asbestos hazards. If ACM may be disturbed during a planned project, a properly trained and accredited person needs to conduct an initial asbestos assessment to determine potential worker exposures and required exposure controls. Asbestos awareness training is required for custodians and school maintenance personnel when ACM is present in the school building (see EPA's Asbestos: School Buildings Web page for more information).*	

References for Priority Issue 4.0 Asbestos:

EPA Asbestos

EPA Asbestos: Asbestos NESHAP

EPA Asbestos: Monitoring Asbestos-Containing Material

EPA Asbestos: School Buildings

EPA Asbestos: State Asbestos Contacts

EPA Asbestos-Containing Materials in Schools; Final Rule and Notice (40 CFR Part 763)

National Institute of Standards and Technology (NIST) National Voluntary Laboratory Accreditation Program (NVLAP): Directory of Accredited
    Laboratories — Asbestos Fiber Analysis (Polarized Light Microscopy Test Method)

NIST NVLAP: Directory of Accredited Laboratories — Asbestos Fiber Analysis (Transmission Electron Microscopy Test Method)

Occupational Safety and Health Administration (OSHA), 29 CFR Part 1926.1101

OSHA, Asbestos

OSHA, Asbestos: Construction

 See Appendix B: Communication and Education   See Appendix C: Worker Protection

ASSESSMENT PROTOCOLS (AP)	MINIMUM ACTIONS (MA)	EXPANDED ACTIONS (EA)
AP 5.1 Assume Lead-Based Paint Is Used in Schools Built Before 1978 Assume there is lead-based paint in schools built before 1978 unless testing shows otherwise. Recognize, however, that lead-based paint may be present in any school. Determine whether paint will be disturbed by the work or the assessment. **AP 5.2 Test Suspect Surfaces That Will Be Disturbed** Three methods may be used. Paint samples may be taken and analyzed by an EPA-accredited laboratory. In addition, a certified risk assessor or inspector may test paint via X-ray fluorescence testing. Finally, in certain circumstances, a certified individual may use an EPA-recognized test kit to determine whether the paint is lead-based. The lead-safe work practices (see Minimum and Expanded Actions) apply unless paint is tested and found not to be lead-based. *Note* *If there are concerns about lead in drinking water, see EPA's Drinking Water in Schools & Child Care Facilities website.*	**MA 5.1 Comply With EPA's Renovation, Repair and Painting (RRP) Program Rule** Among the rule's key elements are the following: • Use a trained and certified renovator employed by a lead-safe certified firm. • Follow lead-safe work practices if disturbing greater than 6 ft² of interior or 20 ft² of exterior painted surfaces. • Contain the work area to avoid occupant exposure. • Minimize lead dust and leave no dust or debris behind. • Clean according to specified protocol and satisfactorily perform cleaning verification or clearance testing. *Note* *Compliance with EPA's RRP Program Rule is required in schools, or portions of schools, where children younger than 6 years of age are present. This Energy Savings Plus Health Guide recommends RRP Program Rule compliance for all schools, regardless of the age of the students or the school.* **MA 5.2 Comply With Local and State Lead Regulations** Comply with local and state regulations that may be applicable to lead hazard-reduction activities and may require additional certified personnel. *Note* *This is not a complete summary of the regulatory requirements. The intent of this Guide is to promote the most health-protective steps that are feasible and practical. The minimum action recommended in this Guide is to comply with whatever the most current version of the RRP Program Rule prescribes and with all local and state regulations that may apply.*	**EA 5.1 Follow Additional Lead-Safe Rehabilitation Practices** Follow additional lead-safe rehabilitation practices, such as the U.S. Department of Housing and Urban Development's (HUD) practices outlined below. In addition to EPA's RRP Program Rule, adhere to the following: • Lower the thresholds for interior painted surface area from 6 ft² to 2 ft². • Require repair of painted surfaces that are disturbed when using lead-safe work practices. • Require meeting lead dust clearance testing standards (as tested by an EPA-certified risk assessor) if more than 2 ft² of paint is disturbed. *Note* *Lead dust clearance testing includes measuring for lead dust on floors, windowsills and window troughs.* **EA 5.2 Replace Windows Containing Lead-Based Paint** Replace windows that test positive for lead-based paint, complying with EPA's RRP Program Rule and other regulations that may be applicable to lead hazard reduction activities. **EA 5.3 Ensure All Paint Used in the Future Is Lead-Free** Some coatings are exempt from lead-containing paint regulations. These include coatings for industrial equipment and those used for building and equipment maintenance coatings. Ensure that all future paint applications in the school are lead-free. See Consumer Product Safety Commission (CPSC) FAQs: Lead In Paint (And Other Surface Coatings).

References for Priority Issue 5.0 Lead:

CPSC FAQs: Lead in Paint (And Other Surface Coatings)
EPA Drinking Water in Schools & Child Care Facilities
EPA Lead: Locate Certified Inspection, Risk Assessment, and Abatement Firms
EPA Lead-Based Paint Renovation, Repair, and Painting Program: Small Entity Compliance Guide to Renovate Right
EPA Locate an RRP Training Class or Provider in Your Area
EPA Recognition of Lead Test Kits
EPA Renovation, Repair, and Painting (RRP) Program
EPA Renovation, Repair, and Painting (RRP) Program: Details on Certification Requirements for Firms
HUD Lead Safe Work Practices
OSHA, Lead

 See Appendix B: Communication and Education   See Appendix C: Worker Protection

ASSESSMENT PROTOCOLS (AP)	MINIMUM ACTIONS (MA)	EXPANDED ACTIONS (EA)

AP 6.1 Determine Whether Fluorescent Light Ballasts Containing PCBs Are Present

Some schools may contain fluorescent light fixtures with ballasts manufactured before 1979 that contain PCBs. Ballasts manufactured between 1978 and 1998 that do not contain PCBs were required to be labeled "No PCBs." Newer fluorescent lighting typically uses electronic ballasts that do not contain PCBs and should be clearly marked as electronic.

If fluorescent light ballasts do not have the statement "No PCBs" or are not marked as electronic, assume that the ballasts contain PCBs or contact the manufacturer to determine whether the ballasts contain PCBs. If the manufacturer is not sure whether the ballasts contain PCBs, assume that they do.

AP 6.2 Assess Caulk That Will Be Disturbed

Assess whether caulk will be disturbed during upgrade activities. Many school buildings built or renovated between 1950 and 1978 have been found to contain PCBs in caulk. Typical locations include around windows, door frames, masonry columns and other masonry materials.

Note

PCBs were not added to caulk after 1978; however, caulk containing PCBs manufactured before 1978 could have been used in buildings after that time.

MA 6.1 Replace PCB-Containing Light Ballasts

Whether PCBs are confirmed or assumed to be present, new lighting fixtures can be used to replace the existing fixtures. PCB-containing light ballasts that are leaking must be replaced and properly disposed of pursuant to EPA regulations. Any oil and stains leaked from PCB-containing ballasts must also be properly cleaned up or disposed of in accordance with the PCB decontamination or disposal regulations. EPA recommends that nonleaking PCB-containing light ballasts also be replaced because of their increased likelihood to fail and leak and because of the increased energy efficiency of new ballasts.

MA 6.2 Properly Dispose of PCB-Containing Light Ballasts

When removing PCB-containing light ballasts, specific notification, packing, reporting, storage, transportation and disposal requirements apply. The EPA PCB-Containing Fluorescent Light Ballasts (FLBs) in School Buildings Web page provides details on managing and disposing of both leaking and nonleaking ballasts, including detailed federal requirements in 40 CFR Part 761 that must be adhered to (disposal, use of containers, proper storage, etc). Ensure that waste management also meets local and state requirements.

Note

Fluorescent light bulbs contain small amounts of mercury. Ensure that the bulbs are handled properly to avoid breakage and release of contaminants. More information on fluorescent bulb disposal requirements may be obtained from your state solid and hazardous waste agencies. See also MA 21.4 Prevent Mercury Exposure.

EA 6.1 Conduct an Assessment for PCBs in Indoor Air and Mitigate as Appropriate

If there are additional concerns about PCBs, consider conducting an IAQ assessment for PCBs following EPA's Compendium Method TO-4A (high air volume) or Compendium Method TO-10A (low air volume). If the air quality test indicates concentrations above EPA's Public Health Levels for PCBs in Indoor School Air, identify potential sources of PCBs and mitigation options. Examples of key mitigation options include ballast and caulk removal, proper ventilation and proper cleaning.

Disposal of caulk or other building products contaminated by PCB-bearing caulk must follow regulatory requirements for PCB waste, as described in 40 CFR Part 761 Subpart D.

Document and store copies of all test results. Include documentation of all sampling locations and disposal measures, including disposal companies used and final destination of waste materials.

 See Appendix B: Communication and Education   See Appendix C: Worker Protection

ASSESSMENT PROTOCOLS (AP)	MINIMUM ACTIONS (MA)	EXPANDED ACTIONS (EA)
	MA 6.3 Address Caulk Potentially Containing PCBs When It Will Be Disturbed During Building Upgrades If PCBs are potentially present in caulk and the caulk will be disturbed during the building renovations (e.g., window or door replacement, improved weatherization sealing), take steps to minimize exposure. Steps to reduce exposure should follow EPA's Current Best Practices for PCBs in Caulk. Schools should also consult the EPA Fact Sheets for Schools and Teachers About PCB-Contaminated Caulk. Disposal of caulk or other building products contaminated by PCB-bearing caulk must follow regulatory requirements for PCB waste, as described in 40 CFR Part 761 Subpart D. Document and store copies of all test results. Include documentation of all sampling locations and disposal measures, including disposal companies used and final destination of waste materials. EPA Regional PCB Coordinators are a resource for all PCB issues.	

References for Priority Issue 6.0 Polychlorinated Biphenyls (PCBs):

EPA Current Best Practices for PCBs in Caulk Fact Sheet - Interim Measures for Assessing Risk and Taking Action to Reduce Exposures
EPA Fact Sheets for Schools and Teachers About PCB-Contaminated Caulk
EPA PCB-Containing Fluorescent Light Ballasts (FLBs) in School Buildings
EPA PCBs in Caulk in Older Buildings
EPA Polychlorinated Biphenyls
EPA Polychlorinated Biphenyls (PCBs) Manufacturing, Processing, Distribution in Commerce, And Use Prohibitions, 40 CFR Part 761
    Subpart D—Storage and Disposal
EPA Public Health Levels for PCBs in Indoor School Air
EPA Recycling Mercury-Containing Light Bulbs (Lamps)
EPA Regional PCB Coordinators
EPA Steps to Safe Renovation and Abatement of Buildings That Have PCB-Containing Caulk
EPA Wastes, Hazardous Wastes, Test Methods, SW-846

Outdoor Contaminants and Sources

	PRIORITY ISSUE 7.0 RADON	
ASSESSMENT PROTOCOLS (AP)	**MINIMUM ACTIONS (MA)**	**EXPANDED ACTIONS (EA)**
AP 7.1 Select a Radon-Testing Professional Qualified measurement professionals are individuals who have demonstrated a minimum degree of appropriate technical knowledge and skills specific to radon testing in large buildings (1) as established in certification requirements of the National Radon Proficiency Program (director@aarst.org) or the National Radon Safety Board (info@nrsb.org) and (2) as required by statute, state licensure or certification program, where applicable. **AP 7.2 Perform Radon Testing Before School Building Modifications** Perform radon testing for the school in accordance with the current applicable standard of practice; such as "Radon Measurement for Schools and Large Buildings" (American National Standards Institute [ANSI]/American Association of Radon Scientists & Technologists, Inc. [AARST] MALB), and state or federal requirements. The standard includes information on which rooms of the school to test, and how and when to conduct testing. Assess the HVAC systems for proper operation prior to and while conducting the initial radon measurements (e.g., ensure that systems are operating as designed with the design minimum amounts of outdoor air ventilation). The current applicable standard of practice, such as in ANSI/AARST MALB, lays out testing options, which are generally dependent upon the device used. **Option 1: Short-Term Test** Because radon levels vary from day-to-day and season-to-season, a short-term test is less likely than a long-term test to provide an average radon level for a school year. A short-term test is the quickest way to test for radon, requiring a period between 2 and 90 days, depending on the device. Short-term testing should be conducted as described in the most current standard of practice.	**MA 7.1 Mitigate High Radon Levels** If the results of radon testing (before or after building modifications) indicate that the average radon levels in parts or all of the school are ≥4 picocuries per liter (pCi/L), take actions to reduce the radon levels, as described in the current version of "Radon Mitigation in Schools and Large Buildings" (ANSI/AARST RMS-LB). Active soil depressurization is the first mitigation method to be considered. Ensure that radon mitigation professionals meet state certification requirements, as applicable, and are certified by either of the groups listed in AP 7.1. **MA 7.2 Ensure HVAC Systems Are Operating Properly** School ventilation systems play a critical role in building performance and must be operating with no less than design minimum outdoor air ventilation rates whenever school rooms are occupied (even if at reduced occupancy) to ensure radon levels are not adversely affected. Decreasing outdoor air ventilation rates will tend to increase radon levels. Thus, a room with radon test results below 4 pCi/L and the HVAC system operating with the design minimum amount of outdoor air ventilation could have elevated radon levels if ventilation is decreased. This is particularly critical for schools without active soil depressurization radon mitigation systems. Outdoor air ventilation should not be decreased below design minimum values when spaces have reduced occupancy, unless radon testing shows that radon levels do not increase above 4 pCi/L when less ventilation is provided. **MA 7.3 Advise Periodic Retesting of Areas That Have Been Mitigated for Radon** Advise school personnel that retesting should be performed according to AP 7.2 and AP 7.3, and ensure that a long-term risk management plan is provided by the mitigation professional in accordance with ANSI/AARST RMS-LB. The plan should contain the essential information that the school needs to conduct basic maintenance and risk management. Ensure that this is included in the written documentation for the renovation project. Retesting should be performed at least every 2 years or according to the risk management plan.	This cell is intentionally blank.

ASSESSMENT PROTOCOLS (AP)	MINIMUM ACTIONS (MA)	EXPANDED ACTIONS (EA)
Option 2: Long-Term Test A long-term test remains in place for more than 90 days, and preferably during the entire school year to give an accurate representation of radon levels at all times of the school year. *Notes* • *Identifying elevated radon levels in a school prior to other building upgrades or renovations will allow radon mitigation systems to be considered and installed as part of the overall building modifications.* • *If a school has previously been tested for radon using appropriate testing protocols as required by the state where the measurements were conducted, or in absence of state requirements, in accordance with the applicable ANSI-approved standard and with no building modifications since the testing, the results may be used for the purposes of this assessment.* • *ANSI/AARST MALB provides a table of steps to take during a radon-testing program, along with detailed descriptions and guidance.* • *Spaces served by demand-controlled ventilation systems may require special attention during radon testing, as these systems allow ventilation rates to vary with occupancy. For radon testing in these spaces, assume a minimum outdoor air ventilation rate based on the minimum expected occupancy.* **AP 7.3 Retest for Radon After School Building Modifications** Retest for radon after all building upgrades and renovations that affect building envelope leakage and airflows are completed, as changes to the building envelope and mechanical systems can affect indoor radon levels.		

References for Priority Issue 7.0 Radon:

ANSI/AARST MALB: Radon Measurement for Schools and Large Buildings (forthcoming)
ANSI/AARST RMS-LB: Radon Mitigation in Schools and Large Buildings (forthcoming)
EPA Radon: State Radon Contact Information

ASSESSMENT PROTOCOLS (AP)	MINIMUM ACTIONS (MA)	EXPANDED ACTIONS (EA)

AP 8.1 Evaluate Potential Sources and Odors

Visually evaluate potential sources and check for odors of gasoline, sewer gas or fuel oil.

AP 8.2 Evaluate the Sewer Vent System

Visually evaluate the integrity of the sewer vent system (e.g., ensure that drain traps have water in them, inspect drain lines for breaks or leaks, check for apparent blockages), particularly if there is sewer gas odor in the school (e.g., during the initial assessment or a fan depressurization test).

AP 8.3 Take Proper Actions if the Odor Source Cannot Be Identified

If an odor is detected but its source cannot be identified, and the school is in a known area of contamination, notify local or state authorities and/or pursue additional assessments before continuing project work.

AP 8.4 Conduct Further Assessment if Contamination Is Suspected

If soil or groundwater contamination is suspected on or near the building site (e.g., former industrial site), volatile contaminants or breakdown products may pose an IAQ risk through soil gas intrusion. In such cases, EPA recommends further assessment before air sealing. Consult your state or tribal voluntary Brownfields cleanup program or environmental regulatory agency for information on the risks of vapor intrusion in your area. EPA's School Siting Guidelines provide information for assessing prior uses of the site and screening for potential environmental hazards, including vapor intrusion. ASTM E2600 describes a tiered approach for screening properties for vapor intrusion and Table X5.1 of the standard provides a list of state vapor-intrusion guidance websites.

Note

A records search of the property and surrounding properties may provide information regarding past uses and spill reports.

MA 8.1 Repair Unattached Sewer Vent System Components

Repair or replace failed or unattached sewer vent system components before proceeding with building upgrade projects.

MA 8.2 Address Drain Traps Prone to Drying Out

If the assessments reveal sewer gas odors from drain traps that are dry because of infrequent use, develop a maintenance plan to periodically add water to the traps to maintain a seal against sewer gases. Consider installing inline drain trap seals to floor drains prone to drying out.

Note

Because of their continuous usage, drain traps in sinks, toilets or drinking fountains seldom are a problem. Usually it is a floor drain in an obscure location, such as the mechanical room, shop area or janitor's closet. Dry drain traps in mechanical rooms are especially problematic because the mechanical rooms often contain heating, cooling and ventilation systems that can quickly spread the gases and odors to other parts of the building. Unitary equipment (e.g., heat pumps) can have dry drain traps, which often results in the undesirable odors being limited to one room.

MA 8.3 Assess and Mitigate Soil Gas Vapor Intrusion

If soil gas vapor intrusion is suspected, assess and mitigate in compliance with local or state standards. Table X5.1 of ASTM E2600 provides a list of state vapor-intrusion guidance websites. If there are no such standards, follow the EPA guidance referenced below for vapor-intrusion evaluation and mitigation.

Note

The causes or sources of contaminants must be identified and corrected before air sealing or other weatherization actions are performed to ensure that the problem is not exacerbated.

EA 8.1 Install Floor Drain Seals to Untrapped Floor Drains

If there are untrapped floor drains, install inline floor drain seals to provide protection against sewer gases.

EA 8.2 Install Automatic Drain Trap Primers

Install automatic drain trap primers, available from several major manufacturers, in drain traps that are susceptible to drying out to ensure that a small amount of water is periodically delivered to the trap.

EA 8.3 Take Proper Measures for Brownfields Sites During New Construction or Building Expansion

Projects located on Brownfields sites (as classified by a federal, state or local government agency) involving new construction or expansion of a ground-level foundation shall include features to prevent migration of soil-gas contaminants into occupied spaces, as described in the ASHRAE Indoor Air Quality Guide, Strategy 3.4.

References for Priority Issue 8.0 Belowground Vapor-Forming Contaminants:

ASHRAE Indoor Air Quality Guide, Strategy 3.4
ASTM E2600-10 Standard Guide for Vapor Encroachment Screening on Property Involved in Real Estate Transactions
EPA Design Tools for Schools: Preventing the Entry of Pollutants from Outside the Building
EPA Engineering Issue: Indoor Air Vapor Intrusion Mitigation Approaches
EPA School Siting Guidelines
EPA Vapor Intrusion

 See Appendix B: Communication and Education

AP 9.1 Investigate Complaints About Motor Vehicle Exhaust Emissions

Ask the school nurse, facilities staff and the school's IAQ coordinator whether there have been occupant complaints regarding vehicle exhaust entering the building. If complaints have been recorded, obtain more information as to when and where complaints originated.

AP 9.2 Identify Air Leaks From Parking Structures

If there are attached or enclosed parking structures, identify the location of air leaks from the parking structures to occupied spaces that might provide pathways for hazardous or irritating emissions to enter occupied spaces. For example, look for doors; overlooking windows; and leaks around walls, doors, windows, ceilings, duct work, air conditioners, and electrical and pipe penetrations.

AP 9.3 Identify and Assess Outdoor Air Intakes

If there are loading docks or vehicle loading/unloading zones (e.g., school bus and parental pick-up areas), identify the location of outdoor air intakes and assess whether they are located an adequate distance away from areas where vehicles may idle. Determine whether these separation distances meet the requirements specified in ASHRAE Standard 62.1, Table 5.5.1.

MA 9.1 Restrict Idling at School Bus Loading/ Unloading Zones, Other Student Pick-Up Areas and Loading Docks

Some local and state governments already have anti-idling laws or policies that must be followed. Otherwise, require engines be shut off (no-idle zone) at school bus loading/unloading zones, parental pick-up areas, loading docks, and other vehicle loading and unloading zones. Provide signage to designate the limits of no idle zones.

MA 9.2 Seal Locations That Separate Parking Structures from Occupied Spaces

Minimize the movement of vehicle exhaust pollutants into the building by air sealing the walls and/or ceilings that separate parking structures from occupied spaces. At a minimum, air seal these locations (if present):

- Leaks into ceiling cavities
  - o First-floor soffits at ceiling level
  - o Single- or two-story roof-wall joints
- Windows: Ensure tight closure and install weather-stripping. If windows currently provide make-up air for corridor or toilet exhaust, new make-up air must be provided to those rooms.
- Doors: Ensure tight closure and install weather-stripping.
- Electrical, plumbing and duct penetrations
- Cracks between masonry or concrete walls and unsealed penetrations
- Leaks in the duct work or air-handler platforms and gaps around the duct work penetrating to the occupied space

MA 9.3 Maintain Positive Pressure in Occupied Spaces Near Parking Structures

Maintain occupied spaces and vestibules at a positive pressure relative to adjacent parking structures. Pressure differentials are typically achieved by using outdoor air; however, to effectively protect IAQ, outdoor air intakes must be located a sufficient distance from potential sources of vehicle exhaust, emergency generator exhaust and other combustion exhausts (see MA 9.6).

A system that uses transfer air from other portions of the building to provide pressurization in spaces near parking structures can be designed, as long as ASHRAE Standard 62.1 outdoor air ventilation requirements also are achieved.

EA 9.1 Relocate Existing Outdoor Air Intakes

If feasible, relocate existing outdoor air intakes away from vehicle exhaust sources to avoid entrainment (see MA 9.7).

EA 9.2 Install Filtration and Air Cleaning for Outdoor Pollutants

Install particle filtration and, in extreme cases, gas-phase air cleaning to treat ventilation air for outdoor pollutants (see EA 18.2 and EA 18.3).

EA 9.3 Add Pressurized Vestibules at All Doorways Connected to Parking Areas

Add a positive-pressure vestibule at each doorway connecting occupied spaces to a parking structure, to provide an airlock.

EA 9.4 Install or Upgrade Exhaust Systems for Vehicle Parking Areas

Install or upgrade exhaust systems for enclosed parking areas:

- Provide adequate exhaust for all localized sources of contamination.
- Maintain sealed exhaust ductwork under a negative pressure in plenum spaces.
- Exhaust to the outdoors, meeting the minimum separation distance requirements of ASHRAE Standard 62.1, Table 5.5.1.

ASSESSMENT PROTOCOLS (AP)	MINIMUM ACTIONS (MA)	EXPANDED ACTIONS (EA)
	MA 9.4 Decouple Areas With Vehicle Exhaust Emissions From Building Air-Handling Systems Eliminate and disconnect supply diffusers and return grilles in garages and vocational classrooms from air-handling systems that serve other occupied spaces. **MA 9.5 Specify Carbon Monoxide Detection and Warning Equipment** Specify the presence of carbon monoxide detection and warning equipment in buildings with attached or enclosed parking structures in accordance with National Fire Protection Association (NFPA) 720 and any applicable local or state requirements (see MA 21.2). **MA 9.6 Locate New Outdoor Air Intakes Away From Vehicle and Generator Exhaust Emissions** Ensure that new outdoor air intakes meet the ASHRAE Standard 62.1, Table 5.5.1 minimum separation distance requirements from any sources of exhaust emissions including the following: • Parking structure exhaust • Local motor vehicle traffic • Vehicle idling areas • Loading docks • Emergency generator exhaust **MA 9.7 Protect Existing Outdoor Air Intakes** If existing outdoor air intakes do not meet the ASHRAE Standard 62.1, Table 5.5.1 separation distance requirements or other local requirements, relocate the intakes if possible. If relocating existing air intakes is cost prohibitive, relocate emission source locations to achieve the required minimum separation distances. **MA 9.8 Use a Vented Heating System for Parking Areas** If heat is needed in the parking structure, use a supplemental heating system that is properly installed and vented to the outdoors.	

References for Priority Issue 9.0 Vehicle Exhaust:

ASHRAE Indoor Air Quality Guide, Strategies 6.2, 6.3 and 6.4
ASHRAE Standard 62.1, Table 5.5.1, Sections 5.2, 5.5 and 5.15
American Transportation Research Institute Compendium of Idling Regulations
EPA Clean School Bus—Idle Reduction Campaign
EPA School Siting Guidelines
NFPA 720: Standard for the Installation of Carbon Monoxide (CO) Detection and Warning Equipment

ASSESSMENT PROTOCOLS (AP)	MINIMUM ACTIONS (MA)	EXPANDED ACTIONS (EA)
AP 10.1 Understand Local and Regional Ambient Air Quality Investigate published information regarding local sources of pollution and regional outdoor air quality, including outdoor ozone levels. ASHRAE Standard 62.1, Section 4 includes a procedure for assessing local and regional outdoor air quality. Regional air quality can be monitored daily on weather websites and at the AirNow website.	**MA 10.1 Meet Outdoor Air Filtration and Air-Cleaning Requirements of ASHRAE Standard 62.1** When the school building is located in an area where the outdoor air exceeds the national standards for particulate matter ($PM_{2.5}$ or PM_{10}) or ozone, ensure that the outdoor air treatment requirements of ASHRAE Standard 62.1, Section 6.2.1 are met for mechanical ventilation systems. This includes the following: • Particulate-matter filters or air-cleaning devices with a Minimum Efficiency Reporting Value (MERV) of at least 6 shall be used in areas where the national standard for PM_{10} is exceeded. • Particulate-matter filters or air-cleaning devices with a MERV of at least 11 shall be used in areas where the national standard for $PM_{2.5}$ is exceeded. • Air-cleaning devices to remove ozone shall be used in areas where the most recent EPA design value exceeds 0.107 ppm. The devices shall have a volumetric ozone-removal efficiency of at least 40% and be operated whenever the outdoor ozone levels are expected to exceed 0.107 ppm. **Note** *At the time ASHRAE Standard 62.1-2013 was published, it identified only four counties in the United States with 8-hour ozone design values exceeding 0.107 ppm, as of July 31, 2013.* Ensure that any increased level of filtration or air cleaning does not create too much static pressure within the HVAC system, which could cause inefficiencies, an increase in energy use or reduced equipment life. For existing systems, check with the manufacturer to determine whether filters with higher MERV ratings can be installed, and install filters with the highest rating that can be accommodated by the equipment.	**EA 10.1 Meet Outdoor Air Filtration and Air-Cleaning Requirements of ASHRAE Standard 189.1** In addition to the requirements of MA 10.1, where the outdoor air exceeds the national standards for $PM_{2.5}$, PM_{10} or ozone, ensure that the outdoor air-filtration and air-cleaning requirements of ASHRAE Standard 189.1, Section 8.3.1.3 are met for mechanical ventilation systems, including the following more stringent criteria: • Particulate-matter filters or air-cleaning devices with a MERV of at least 8 shall be used in areas where the national standard for PM_{10} is exceeded. • Particulate-matter filters or air-cleaning devices with a MERV of at least 13 shall be used in areas where the national standard for $PM_{2.5}$ is exceeded. • Air-cleaning devices to remove ozone must be provided and used for schools that are located in areas that are in "nonattainment" with the National Ambient Air Quality Standards for ozone. The removal efficiency of the system shall be at least equal to what is required under MA 10.1.

References for Priority Issue 10.0 Local and Regional Ambient Air Quality:

ASHRAE Indoor Air Quality Guide, Strategy 3.1Standard 62.1, Sections 4 and 6.2.1
ASHRAE Standard 189.1, Section 8.3.1.3
EPA Air Trends
EPA AirNow
EPA National Ambient Air Quality Standards

 See Appendix B: Communication and Education

ASSESSMENT PROTOCOLS (AP)	MINIMUM ACTIONS (MA)	EXPANDED ACTIONS (EA)

AP 11.1 Identify Potential Pests and Integrated Pest Management (IPM) Resources

Identify pests likely to colonize the building based on project location. Identify and acquire resources to assist with implementing IPM (e.g., state/county extension, publications and online resources, nongovernmental organizations, pest management professionals with expertise in school IPM), including the proper identification of pests.

AP 11.2 Identify Evidence of Pests

Identify evidence of pests (e.g., rodents, squirrels, termites, birds, bats, cockroaches). Note the location and identify pest-contaminated materials. Determine whether pesticides (rodenticides, insecticides, herbicides, fungicides) are presently being used. See MA 11.1 for minimum actions to address pest infestations.

Notes

- *Areas that have a significant potential for pest infestations include attics, basements, crawlspaces, and around chimneys, mechanical stacks and plumbing cleanouts.*

- *Termites and some other types of pest infestations often are an indication of moisture problems. See Priority Issue 3.0 Moisture Control and Mold for diagnosing moisture problems.*

AP 11.3 Assess Whether the School Has an IPM Plan

Consult the school facilities staff and IAQ coordinator to determine whether the school has an IPM plan and the degree to which the plan is being followed. Refer to EPA's *Integrated Pest Management in Schools* brochure and Web page for more information.

MA 11.1 Mitigate Pest Infestations

If there is indication of current or past pest infestations within the building, seek assistance from a professional who ensures IPM practices with his or her pest management services (some examples may include Greenpro, Greenshield or equivalently certified IPM professionals).

Determine whether pesticides will need to be used and follow the school district's Pest Management Plan/Policy for pest control. Whenever pesticides are applied, the pesticide label must be followed, as it is the law.

Consider providing signage to communicate when pesticide applications will occur. The signage should be posted prior to the application (e.g., 1 week) and include dates when the application will take place. Encourage scheduling pesticide applications when school is not in session.

Do not begin work in pest-infested zones until infested materials are properly removed. In some cases, professional assistance may be needed to remove infested materials.

Note

Many states require that pest management professionals be licensed.

MA 11.2 Patch Openings in Areas of Rodent Infestation

In areas with evidence of rodent infestation, patch and seal exterior holes that are larger than 1/4" by 3/8" with pest-resistant materials (e.g., copper mesh, hardware cloth, sheet metal, concrete) before applying weatherization materials that may be susceptible to gnawing by rodents (e.g., caulk, foam or insulation).

MA 11.3 Reduce Potential for Pest Entry

Block, seal and eliminate pest entry points around the building envelope. Examples include gaps around doors and windows; between the foundation and the upper portion of the building; and around utility pipes, conduits and wires.

EA 11.1 Use Sealable Exterior Garbage Containers

Ensure that exterior garbage cans and dumpsters are sealable and sanitized regularly.

EA 11.2 Pest Resistant Kitchen Design

Follow design guidance outlined for institutional kitchens in the San Francisco Department of the Environment (SF Environment) Pest Prevention by Design document.

ASSESSMENT PROTOCOLS (AP)	MINIMUM ACTIONS (MA)	EXPANDED ACTIONS (EA)
	MA 11.4 Block Pest Movement Through Building Reduce risk of pest dispersal throughout the building by sealing and blocking passageways that pests can use to move freely to obtain food, water and harborage. This includes gaps around floor and ceiling joists; penetrations in walls, floors and ceilings; and openings around shafts and chutes. **MA 11.5 Protect Outdoor Air Intakes and Exhausts** Protect air intakes from bird and pest entry (e.g., cover openings with corrosion-resistant ½-inch screen or galvanized mesh). Similarly, protect exhaust vents from rodent, bird and pest entry (e.g., cover openings with louvers). Avoid creating conditions that can clog exhaust vents. Advise facility managers to regularly inspect, clean and repair screens or louvers over air intakes and exhausts (e.g., at least semi-annually or when replacing HVAC filters). Make sure that rooftop air handlers are air sealed to their roof curbs to reduce pest entry. **MA 11.6 Maintain Existing Pest Protections** Do not disturb or eliminate any building-related materials that are in place to exclude pests. **MA 11.7 Keep Vegetation and Clutter Away From Building and Mechanical Systems Components** Remove clutter, eliminate wood piles and waste near the building, and remove any bushes, trees or other vegetation within 2 feet of the structure. Keep vegetation away from outdoor air intakes and outdoor mechanical equipment. Do not pile soil or mulch against the building's exterior walls. **MA 11.8 School IPM Plan** Ensure that the school has an IPM plan. Refer to EPA's *Integrated Pest Management in Schools* brochure and website for more information. The IPM checklist provided in EPA's *IAQ Tools for Schools* Action Kit also can be used as an example. Preventive IPM measures are easy to implement and often improve the overall maintenance of the school. These measures can include the following: • Maintaining good sanitation practices • Installing high-density door sweeps • Restricting areas in which food is eaten • Moving dumpsters and food disposal containers away from the school, and maintaining the containers in good condition • Pressure-cleaning food service areas • Sealing cracks and crevices • Cleaning gutters and directing water flow away from building to prevent saturation A successful IPM program takes advantage of all pest management strategies, including prevention, inspection, communication, biopesticide use, and judicious and careful use of pesticides when necessary. Follow IPM guidelines for roach control and consider using baits over broadcast applications when possible, to reduce possible pesticide exposure.	

References for Priority Issue 11.0 Pests:

ASHRAE Indoor Air Quality Guide, Strategy 3.6
CDC Resource on Rodents
EPA *IAQ Tools for Schools* Action Kit: Integrated Pest Management Background and Checklist
EPA Integrated Pest Management in Schools Brochure and Website
SF Department of Environment Pest Prevention by Design Guidelines
U.S. Department of Agriculture Cooperative Extension System Offices

ASSESSMENT PROTOCOLS (AP)	MINIMUM ACTIONS (MA)	EXPANDED ACTIONS (EA)
AP 12.1 Inspect Floor Surfaces at Building Entrances Inspect all building entrances for walk-off mats or entry mat systems. Note accumulation of dirt or moisture on interior floors near building entrances that might indicate need for walk-off mats or entryway floor-cleaning systems.	**MA 12.1 Provide Walk-Off Mats** Provide walk-off mats to trap dirt and moisture at all building entrances. The mats need to be long enough to allow at least five full steps for people entering the school (a minimum of 10 feet long). Walk-off mats should be regularly vacuumed and cleaned according to manufacturer's printed instructions. Mats should have anti-slip backings or other means to reduce sliding and tripping hazards. Mats should not be placed over carpeted areas and should have an impervious, readily cleanable surface beneath them. ***Note*** *Mats should be periodically moved and allowed to dry. Mats in high-traffic areas and over vinyl flooring should be moved and allowed to dry frequently during wet weather conditions (e.g., on a daily basis).* **MA 12.2 Follow EPA Guidance on Cleanliness and Maintenance in Schools** Provide a copy of the EPA *IAQ Tools for Schools* Action Kit: Building and Grounds Maintenance Checklist to the facility manager.	**EA 12.1 Install Permanent Entryway Systems** Install permanent entryway systems at all regularly used building entrances to capture dirt and moisture, in accordance with ASHRAE Standard 189.1, Section 8.3.1.5 or EPA's *IAQ Design Tools for Schools,* Entry Mat Barriers. The entry mat system should— • Provide a scraper surface, an absorption surface and a finishing surface, in sequence in the direction of travel into the building. • Be as wide as the entry doors. • Have anti-slip backings or other locking mechanisms to reduce sliding and tripping hazards. • Be designed for regular cleaning to remove accumulated dirt. • Not be installed over an existing walk-off mat or other entryway system.

References for Priority Issue 12.0 Tracked-In Pollutants:

ASHRAE Indoor Air Quality Guide, Strategy 3.5
ASHRAE Standard 189.1, Section 8.3.1.5
Association of Physical Plant Administrators Operational Guidelines for Educational Facilities: Custodial
EPA IAQ Design *Tools for Schools*, Entry Mat Barriers
EPA *IAQ Tools for Schools* Action Kit: Building and Grounds Maintenance Background and Checklist

 See Appendix B: Communication and Education

Indoor Contaminants and Sources

ASSESSMENT PROTOCOLS (AP)	MINIMUM ACTIONS (MA)	EXPANDED ACTIONS (EA)
AP 13.1 Review Content and Emissions Documentation for New Products Review information on the chemical content and emissions for products being considered for purchase and installation during the building upgrade project to determine whether they contain potentially hazardous compounds. Many of these products and materials (e.g., plywood, particle board, pressed wood, insulation, paints, sealants, cleaning supplies) may contain VOCs or other hazardous compounds to which exposure should be minimized or eliminated during and after the project.	**MA 13.1 Select Least Toxic Materials** When installing new products and materials, use the least toxic product or material feasible to effectively do the job. For example, use products and materials that indicate they have (or are certified as having) low-VOC content or low-VOC emissions and follow manufacturers' printed instructions for use. Specify products and materials that meet independent certification and testing protocols, such as the following: • California Department of Public Health, Emission Testing Method for California Specification 01350, complying with the limit requirements for classrooms, regardless of space type • Carpet and Rug Institute Green Label Plus program criteria, or equivalent standards for carpet • Collaborative for High Performance Schools High Performance Products Database • Green Seal Standard GS-11 • Greenguard Gold Certification Program • Master Painters Institute Green Performance Standards X-Green, GPS-1 or GPS-2 • Resilient Floor Covering Institute, FloorScore • Scientific Certification Systems Standard EC-10.2-2007, Indoor Advantage Gold • Insulation products that contain no added formaldehyde and are moisture resistant • Ceiling tiles with low formaldehyde emission rates	**EA 13.1 Air Out New Materials** Where possible, air out new materials in a well-ventilated, clean and dry space prior to installation. Off-site opening of wrapped or tightly packaged materials to facilitate this conditioning step is also acceptable. **EA 13.2 Seal Composite Wood Products** Seal composite wood products (e.g., particle board, pressed wood) that are not compliant with California Title 17 Airborne Toxic Control Measures (ATCM) or that do not meet Section 6.1 of EPA's Indoor airPLUS Construction Specifications with a sealant intended to reduce VOC emissions. Seal all exposed surfaces and holes, as appropriate. Check with vendors for recommendations on sealing their engineered wood products. **EA 13.3 Investigate and Correct Contaminant Source Problems After Building Modifications** If odors or complaints indicate VOCs or other airborne contaminants after work has been completed, remove any potential sources (e.g., arts and crafts materials, fiberglass that may contain formaldehyde) from the room or area. If removal is not feasible, consider installing local exhaust ventilation for sources that are isolated to a specific room or area, at least on a temporary basis until materials off-gassing has subsided. If these actions do not solve the problem (e.g., persistent odors, occupant complaints), hiring an environmental professional and testing may be necessary.

ASSESSMENT PROTOCOLS (AP)	MINIMUM ACTIONS (MA)	EXPANDED ACTIONS (EA)

MA 13.2 Use Low-Emitting Wood and Composite-Wood Products

When installing structural plywood or pressed or composite wood products, select those that are certified compliant with California Title 17 ATCM to reduce formaldehyde emissions from composite wood products. If California Title 17 ATCM compliant materials are not available, use wood products that meet Section 6.1 of EPA's Indoor airPLUS Construction Specifications or composite wood products that contain no added formaldehyde.

Notes

• *California Title 17 ATCM regulations require reduced formaldehyde emissions from composite wood products and finished goods that contain composite wood products sold, offered for sale, supplied, used or manufactured for sale in California.*

• *Title VI of TSCA sets national formaldehyde emission standards for composite wood products that are identical to California's Phase II emission standards. EPA currently is developing the regulations to implement these standards nationally.*

MA 13.3 Provide Adequate Ventilation

Ensure that the school meets the Minimum Actions in Priority Issues 19.0 Outdoor Air Ventilation and 20.0 Exhaust Ventilation.

MA 13.4 Post-Construction Flush-Out With Outdoor Air

After construction is completed, ventilate the renovated building/spaces with the design outdoor air ventilation rates before occupancy resumes. Ensure that HVAC systems are operational and capable of adequately controlling indoor humidity levels during the flush out. Do not conduct a "bake-out" in an attempt to reduce VOC emissions after the building is occupied, because it may cause VOCs to be absorbed by other interior materials and may damage building components.

If possible, follow the post-construction flush-out requirements specified in ASHRAE Standard 189.1, Section 10.3.1.4(b), which requires a total number of air changes corresponding to the ventilation system operating at its design outdoor air flow rate continuously, 24 hours per day for 14 days. A longer flush-out period can be used if there are concerns or complaints about IAQ after the initial flush out. Additional, periodic flush out may also be needed for spaces that have intermittent or infrequent occupancy and are not ventilated for extended periods.

MA 13.5 Limit VOC Absorption During Construction

Follow guidance outlined in MA 22.3 to protect absorptive materials during construction.

MA 13.6 Limit Children's and Other Occupants' Exposure

Follow Priority Issue 22.0 Protecting IAQ During Construction to protect children and other occupants from material emissions during building upgrades.

EA 13.4 Post-Construction Flush-Out or Post-Construction Baseline IAQ Monitoring Per ASHRAE Standard 189.1

After construction is completed, meet the requirements of ASHRAE Standard 189.1, Section 10.3.1.4(b) for either a flush-out or baseline IAQ monitoring before occupancy is resumed in the renovated school/spaces. A flush-out period longer than specified in ASHRAE Standard 189.1 can be used if there are concerns or complaints about IAQ after the initial flush out. Additional, periodic flush out may also be needed for spaces that have intermittent or infrequent occupancy and are not ventilated for extended periods.

EA 13.5 Promote Transparency of Chemical Constituents in Products and Materials

To promote transparency of chemical constituents associated with the manufacture of a product and substances residing in the final product, require products that have submitted their complete chemical inventory to a third-party for verification. Make the verification/certification by the third-party publicly available.

References for Priority Issue 13.0 Building Products/Materials Emissions:

ASHRAE Indoor Air Quality Guide, Strategies 5.1 and 5.2
ASHRAE Standard 189.1, Sections 10.3.1.4 and 10.3.1.4 (b) 1
California Department of Public Health, Emission Testing Method for California Specification 01350
California Title 17 ATCM to Reduce Formaldehyde Emissions from Composite Wood Products
Carpet and Rug Institute Green Label Plus
Collaborative for High Performance Schools High Performance Products Database
EPA Formaldehyde Emissions From Composite Wood Products
EPA An Introduction to Indoor Air Quality: Volatile Organic Compounds
EPA *IAQ Design Tools for Schools*, Controlling Pollutants and Sources
EPA Indoor airPLUS Construction Specifications
Green Seal Standard GS-11
Greenguard Gold Certification Program
Master Painters Institute Green Performance Standards X-Green, GPS-1 or GPS-2
Resilient Floor Covering Institute, FloorScore
Scientific Certification Systems Standard EC-10.2-2007, Environmental Certification Program, Indoor Air Quality Performance
TSCA Title VI – Formaldehyde Standards for Composite Wood Products

ASSESSMENT PROTOCOLS (AP)	MINIMUM ACTIONS (MA)	EXPANDED ACTIONS (EA)

AP 14.1 Complete a Safety Inspection

Complete a safety inspection of all vented combustion appliances in the school (e.g., furnaces, boilers, space heaters, water heaters). The inspection shall include observations for applicable code requirements including proper clearances, condition of venting, assessment of the potential for back drafting, integrity of fuel lines, and safety of electrical connections and the appliance itself.

For gas-fired appliances and equipment, make this assessment using applicable installation standards, including the National Fuel Gas Code, ANSI Z223.1/NFPA 54, the applicable ANSI Z21/Z83 gas-fired appliance safety standards and the manufacturer's printed instructions. Determine whether gas-fired appliance installations comply with Section 9.3 "Air for Combustion and Ventilation" of ANSI Z223.1/NFPA 54 for proper venting, including influences of other building ventilation and exhausting equipment.

For oil-fired appliances and equipment, make this assessment using applicable installation standards, including the Standard for the Installation of Oil-Burning Equipment, ANSI/NFPA 31, the applicable ANSI/UL oil-fired appliance safety standard, and the manufacturer's printed instructions.

MA 14.1 Test, Repair, Remove or Replace Combustion Appliances

Complete all applicable actions under the Assessment Protocols and ensure compliance with applicable codes and standards. Test combustion appliances for proper draft and venting under worst-case conditions before and after work that affects envelope leakage and airflows (e.g., air sealing, insulation, addition or upgrade of exhaust fans). Repair, remove or replace combustion equipment and address other issues or deficiencies as needed to meet the applicable codes and standards.

Note

All equipment removals should include proper disposal so that hazardous units are not reinstalled or used elsewhere.

Address depressurization and potential back drafting problems (e.g., with combustion make-up air, fan interlocks, transfer grilles, jumper ducts, louvered doors or door undercuts) or, with the school's permission, disable the exhaust equipment causing the problems provided it does not conflict with the specific exhaust requirements for spaces served by the exhaust equipment. Ensure that combustion appliances are installed with sufficient access for proper maintenance and are operating in compliance with the original manufacturer's printed specifications.

MA 14.2 Ensure Proper Exhaust Locations

Ensure that combustion exhaust is captured as close to the combustion source as possible, exhausted directly outdoors, and not vented into other indoor spaces such as attics, crawlspaces or basements.

MA 14.3 Ensure Adequate Make-Up Air

Ensure that vented appliances have sufficient make-up air to replace vented air and maintain normal operating conditions.

MA 14.4 Ensure Proper Boiler Operation

Ensure that boiler firing adjustments are working properly so that soot is not dispelled out of the atmospheric dampers into boiler rooms. Confirm that boilers do not release black smoke through the chimney for more than a very brief period.

MA 14.5 Verify Installation of Carbon Monoxide Detection and Warning Equipment

Ensure that carbon monoxide detection and warning equipment is installed and meets the requirements of NFPA 720 and any applicable local or state requirements.

EA 14.1 Install Power-Vented or Sealed-Combustion Equipment

If replacing combustion equipment located in occupied or conditioned spaces, recommend power-vented or sealed-combustion equipment. Install new combustion equipment in accordance with the Air Conditioning Contractors of America's (ACCA) Standard 5.

 See Appendix B: Communication and Education

References for Priority Issue 14.0 Vented Combustion Appliances:

ACCA Standard 5 QI-2010: HVAC Quality Installation Specification
ANSI Z223.1/NFPA 54 National Fuel Gas Code
ANSI Z21/Canadian Standards Association (CSA) and ANSI Z83/CSA Series, Products and Standards for Gas, Oil and Solid Fuel
   Appliances and Equipment
ASHRAE Indoor Air Quality Guide, Strategies 6.1 and 6.2
ASHRAE Standard 62.1, Section 5.7
NFPA 31: Standard for Installation of Oil-Burning Equipment
NFPA 211: Standard for Chimneys, Fireplaces, Vents, and Solid Fuel-Burning Appliances
NFPA 720: Standard for the Installation of Carbon Monoxide (CO) Detection and Warning Equipment

ASSESSMENT PROTOCOLS (AP)	MINIMUM ACTIONS (MA)	EXPANDED ACTIONS (EA)
AP 15.1 Identify Unvented Combustion Appliances and Applicable Regulations Identify any unvented gas or kerosene space heaters or vent-free combustion appliances (e.g., ovens, ranges, lab equipment, space heaters). Determine whether any local or state regulations prohibiting these devices apply.	**MA 15.1 Ensure Adequate Ventilation and Exhaust in Spaces With Unvented Combustion Equipment (Other Than Heaters)** Ensure that ASHRAE Standard 62.1 requirements for outdoor air ventilation and exhaust are met for each specific room where unvented combustion equipment is used. The following unvented equipment is typically found in schools, and each has specific ventilation and exhaust requirements, per ASHRAE Standard 62.1. • Food preparation devices, such as ovens and ranges that are operated to prepare food for onsite consumption or to train students in the culinary arts • Unvented combustion devices used in laboratories and classrooms for educational and vocational purposes (e.g., gas burners, Bunsen burners, propane torches) • Unvented combustion equipment used in schools for custodial and maintenance purposes (e.g., natural gas- or propane-powered floor maintenance equipment, forklifts, and tractors) Ensure rooms where carbon monoxide is likely to be generated (e.g., kitchens, science laboratories, vocational classrooms) are operated at a negative pressure relative to surrounding areas. Ensure that negative pressures in kitchens induced by exhaust fans do not exceed NFPA 96 Section 8.3.1 guidelines resulting from a lack of make-up air. **MA 15.2 Remove Unvented Combustion Space Heaters** With the school's permission, remove any unvented gas or kerosene space heaters that do not conform to local or state regulations. If the heaters are used as the primary source of heat for a space, replace them with electric or vented, code-compliant heating systems. With the school's permission, remove other unvented heaters, except when used as a secondary heat source and it can be confirmed that the unit is in compliance with ANSI Z21.11.2. Advise the school staff to always follow the manufacturer's printed instructions for proper operation and maintenance. *Note* *All equipment removals should include proper disposal so that hazardous units are not reinstalled or used elsewhere.* **MA 15.3 Verify Installation of Carbon Monoxide Detection and Warning Equipment** Ensure carbon monoxide detection and warning equipment is installed and meets the requirements of NFPA 720 and any applicable local or state requirements.	This cell is intentionally blank.

References for Priority Issue 15.0 Unvented Combustion Appliances:

ANSI Z21.11.2 Gas-Fired Room Heaters Volume II, Unvented Room Heaters
ASHRAE Standard 62.1
EPA IAQ: Guidance on Carbon Monoxide
NFPA 96 Standard for Ventilation Control and Fire Protection of Commercial Cooking Operations
NFPA 720: Standard for the Installation of Carbon Monoxide (CO) Detection and Warning Equipment

 See Appendix B: Communication and Education

ASSESSMENT PROTOCOLS (AP)	MINIMUM ACTIONS (MA)	EXPANDED ACTIONS (EA)
AP 16.1 Identify Indoor Sources of Ozone Determine whether there are or will be significant sources of ozone generation in the building, including photocopiers and laser printers. Determine whether any air-cleaning or purifying equipment designed to intentionally produce ozone is present (e.g., ozone generators and air purifiers).	**MA 16.1 Avoid Ozone-Generating Air-Cleaning Equipment** Do not install air-cleaning or air-purifying equipment designed to intentionally produce ozone (i.e., ozone generators). Recommend removal of existing air-cleaning or air-purifying equipment designed to intentionally produce ozone, if present. **MA 16.2 Provide Adequate Ventilation and Exhaust in Areas with Ozone-Generating Office Equipment** Ventilate and exhaust printing, copying, and reprographics areas and other areas with office equipment that emits ozone in accordance with ASHRAE Standard 62.1 and the printed guidelines provided by the equipment manufacturer.	**EA 16.1 Test Existing Office Equipment for Ozone Emissions and Mitigate Elevated Levels** Test for ozone emissions from existing office equipment following ASTM D6670. Repair or remove office equipment that is found to emit ozone at a level greater than 0.02 milligrams per cubic meter. **EA 16.2 Install Ozone Capture/Removal Systems** Recommend purchasing office-equipment fitted with an active carbon filter or other ozone absorption device or fitted with a dedicated exhaust and heat removal system. These often are options available from equipment manufacturers.

References for Priority Issue 16.0 Ozone from Indoor Sources:

ASHRAE Standard 62.1

ASTM International D6670-13 Standard Practice for Full-Scale Chamber Determination of Volatile Organic Emissions from Indoor Materials/Products

California EPA Air Resources Board: Hazardous Ozone-Generating 'Air Purifiers'

EPA Ozone Generators that Are Sold as Air Cleaners

 See Appendix B: Communication and Education

ASSESSMENT PROTOCOLS (AP)	MINIMUM ACTIONS (MA)	EXPANDED ACTIONS (EA)
AP 17.1 Assess Smoking Policy Federal law prohibits smoking within any indoor facility regularly or routinely used for kindergarten, elementary, or secondary education or library service to children. Local or state laws may be more restrictive. Determine whether the school has a policy that prohibits smoking inside the school. Determine whether there are locations where outdoor smoking is allowed on school grounds and the distances of these locations from the building's entrances, outdoor air intakes and operable windows. **AP 17.2 Identify Occupant Complaints About Smoking** Ask the school nurse and the school's IAQ coordinator whether there have been occupant complaints about smoking odors.	**MA 17.1 Ensure the School Has a Policy on Tobacco Use** Any school policy on tobacco use must be consistent with local, state and federal laws. The policy should include prohibitions against tobacco use by students, all school staff, parents and visitors on school property, in school vehicles, and at school-sponsored functions away from school property. If there are designated outdoor smoking locations, ensure that these locations are a minimum of 25 feet from all building entrances, outdoor air intakes and operable windows. ***Note*** *Federal law prohibits smoking inside school buildings. It is strongly suggested that the school tobacco use policy also prohibit smoking on school grounds and in school vehicles.*	This cell is intentionally blank.

References for Priority Issue 17.0 Environmental Tobacco Smoke:

ASHRAE Standard 189.1, Section 8.3.1.4
CDC Guidelines for School Health Programs to Prevent Tobacco Use and Addiction
EPA IAQ Tools for Schools: IAQ Reference Guide, Appendix F—Secondhand Smoke
United States Code, Title 20, Chapter 68, Section 6083: Nonsmoking policy for children's services

 See Appendix B: Communication and Education

Heating, Ventilation and Air Conditioning (HVAC)

PRIORITY ISSUE 18.0 HVAC EQUIPMENT

ASSESSMENT PROTOCOLS (AP)	MINIMUM ACTIONS (MA)	EXPANDED ACTIONS (EA)
AP 18.1 Conduct HVAC Assessment Evaluate the condition of the existing HVAC system components in accordance with minimum inspection standards of ASHRAE/ACCA Standard 180, ASHRAE handbooks, or other equivalent standards and guidelines. The HVAC assessment is to include an evaluation of whether the system is functioning properly, based on ASHRAE and ACCA standards appropriate for the type of equipment. Determine whether the HVAC system is properly sized in accordance with ASHRAE load calculation manuals and handbooks or other equivalent standardized guidelines. Evaluate building heating and cooling loads after planned modifications and HVAC equipment capacities for sensible and latent loads. If HVAC replacement or modification is anticipated, base sizing calculations on post-upgrade conditions. The assessment shall include the following: • Inspect the air filters and filtration system for overall filter condition, filter efficiency, particle accumulation, filter blow out, and air leakage around filters. • Inspect air plenums and ductwork for indications of mold growth, excess dirt or obstructions. Determine whether components and systems installed in plenums (e.g., cables) are rated for use in plenum spaces. • Inspect exhaust system for proper direction of fan rotation, corrosion, excessive vibration, blockage, or pressure differentials that can lead to leakage or flow reversals.	**MA 18.1 Ensure Existing Systems Operate Properly** Based on an assessment of equipment condition and sizing, repair, modify or replace equipment to ensure proper HVAC function and correct related deficiencies. The ability to modify and adjust the existing HVAC system may be limited by its initial design. Review the original equipment specifications and seek outside engineering assistance as needed. If maintenance, cleaning or repairs are needed to restore the HVAC to proper functioning, perform them in accordance with ASHRAE/ACCA Standard 180, ACCA Standard 6, or other equivalent standards and guidelines. Ensure that there is a scheduled inspection and maintenance program for HVAC systems in accordance with ASHRAE/ACCA Standard 180. For units with filter status pressure switches, ensure that switches are operating properly and scheduled for regular calibrations. When adjusting existing HVAC systems, refer to Priority Issues 19.0 Outdoor Air Ventilation and 20.0 Exhaust Ventilation for guidance on ventilation and exhaust requirements. **MA 18.2 Properly Size and Install New HVAC Equipment** If replacing equipment, base sizing calculations on post-upgrade project conditions. Install new equipment in accordance with ACCA Standard 5 and verify installation in accordance with ACCA Standard 9, ASHRAE handbooks or other equivalent standards and guidelines. **MA 18.3 Ensure MERV 8 Filters in New HVAC Systems** Ensure that new HVAC systems have a minimum MERV 8 filter, located upstream of all cooling coils or other devices with wetted surfaces, in accordance with ASHRAE Standard 62.1 requirements. There shall be no air bypass around the filters and no air cleaners designed to intentionally produce ozone.	**EA 18.1 Install Higher Efficiency Filters in New HVAC Systems** Use higher efficiency filters upstream of all cooling coils or other devices with wetted surfaces (e.g., MERV 11 or higher), if the new equipment is capable of physically accommodating the filters and has adequate fan capacity to overcome the high-efficiency filters' pressure drop. **EA 18.2 Increase Filter Efficiencies in Existing HVAC Systems** For existing systems, check with the manufacturer to determine whether filters with higher MERV ratings can be installed without introducing an unacceptable increase in airflow resistance. Install filters with the highest MERV rating that can be accommodated by the equipment. Review original equipment specifications and seek outside engineering assistance as needed. **EA 18.3 Employ Filtration and Air Cleaning To Supplement Source Control and Ventilation** Install filtration and gas-phase air cleaning strategies, if appropriate, to supplement pollutant source control strategies and the performance of the outdoor air ventilation system in removing pollutants. Maintain the prescribed minimum outdoor air ventilation rates if this approach is used (see Priority Issue 19.0). Consider the limitations of the air handling system, the amount and severity of contaminants, and the features of the filtration and air cleaning equipment. Filtration and air cleaning strategies may be advisable in the following conditions: • Outdoor air often is polluted (e.g., schools located near roadways) or consistently/seasonally burdened with high heat or humidity. • Source control tactics are insufficient or occupant activities generate high contaminant loads. • Occupants require enhanced protection from contaminants.

 See Appendix B: Communication and Education   See Appendix C: Worker Protection

ASSESSMENT PROTOCOLS (AP)	MINIMUM ACTIONS (MA)	EXPANDED ACTIONS (EA)
	MA 18.4 Remediate Mold in Air Plenums and Ductwork If mold is found in air plenums or ductwork during the HVAC assessment, follow the guidance outlined in MA 3.2. **MA 18.5 Control Bacterial Growth in HVAC Systems and Mechanical Equipment** Follow OSHA Technical Manual: Legionnaires' Disease to protect against bacteria growth in cooling towers, evaporative condensers, humidifiers, hot water systems that operate below 140 °F, fire sprinkler systems, ice machines, and warm-water piping for eye wash and safety showers. *Note* *ASHRAE has a proposed new standard under development, Standard 188P, "Legionellosis: Risk Management for Building Water Systems." The new standard will provide minimum legionellosis risk management requirements for the design, construction, commissioning, operation, maintenance, repair, replacement and expansion of new and existing buildings and their associated water systems and components. When this standard is published, its requirements will be considered a Minimum Action in this Energy Savings Plus Health Guide.*	

References for Priority Issue References for Priority Issue 18.0 HVAC Equipment:

ACCA Standard 5 QI-2010: HVAC Quality Installation Specification
ACCA Standard 6-2007: Restoring the Cleanliness of HVAC Systems
ACCA Standard 9 QIVP-2011: HVAC Quality Installation Verification Protocols
ASHRAE/ACCA Standard 180
ASHRAE *Handbook: Fundamentals*
ASHRAE *Handbook: HVAC Applications*
ASHRAE *Indoor Air Quality Guide*, Strategy 7.5
ASHRAE *Load Calculations Application Manual*
ASHRAE Standard 62.1, Section 5.8
ASHRAE Standard 188P (forthcoming)
ASHRAE Standard 189.1, Section 8.3.1.3.a.1
OSHA Technical Manual: Legionnaires' Disease

ASSESSMENT PROTOCOLS (AP)	MINIMUM ACTIONS (MA)	EXPANDED ACTIONS (EA)

AP 19.1 Determine Compliance With ASHRAE Standard 62.1 Ventilation Requirements

Based on existing design documents and balancing reports, or building audit results, determine whether the school complies with the ventilation requirements of ASHRAE Standard 62.1. This will require measuring airflows onsite.

Note

Some existing ventilation systems may not be capable of meeting the minimum outdoor air ventilation requirements of ASHRAE Standard 62.1 because of capacity limitations, whereas other existing ventilation systems may have sufficient capacity to meet or exceed the standard.

ASHRAE Standard 62.1, Table 6.2.2.1 provides minimum breathing zone ventilation requirements for various space types. The Ventilation Rate Procedure requires that zone and system ventilation rates be calculated based on these minimum rates. Each ventilation zone and each system must meet the ASHRAE requirements for the building to be in compliance.

Determine whether the ventilation system satisfies the requirements of ASHRAE Standard 62.1, Section 5 for Systems and Equipment.

MA 19.1 Adjust Existing Systems To Meet ASHRAE Standard 62.1 Where Possible

Adjust the ventilation rates of existing systems to meet the requirements of ASHRAE Standard 62.1, where possible, using the Ventilation Rate Procedure.

If it is not possible to increase ventilation rates to meet the requirements of ASHRAE Standard 62.1 because of equipment capacity limitations, building space limitations, budgetary constraints or other reasons, the ventilation system shall be adjusted to provide the maximum outdoor airflow possible. The conditions (e.g., heating and cooling loads) for which the systems cannot meet the ASHRAE Standard 62.1 requirements should be identified, and the systems should be operated to meet the ASHRAE Standard 62.1 requirements whenever load conditions permit.

Note

ASHRAE Standard 62.1 also allows a Natural Ventilation Procedure in conjunction with mechanical ventilation systems, with a few specified exceptions. When natural ventilation is provided, efforts should be made to ensure that windows and other ventilation openings are operated appropriately.

Ensure compliance with Section 5 of ASHRAE Standard 62.1 wherever possible.

MA 19.2 Consider Impacts of Building Envelope Air Sealing on Ventilation

Avoid tightening the building envelope to reduce air exchange rates if mechanical ventilation rates are deficient. Ensure that school buildings relying on natural ventilation will have adequate ventilation after weatherization activities.

EA 19.1 Replace/Upgrade Existing Systems To Meet ASHRAE Standard 62.1

If existing systems cannot meet ASHRAE Standard 62.1, upgrade HVAC systems to obtain compliance or create a system upgrade plan to meet ASHRAE Standard 62.1 during future upgrades.

EA 19.2 Install Monitoring To Ensure Adequate Outdoor Air Ventilation

For mechanical ventilation applications, install permanent outdoor airflow monitoring systems in accordance with ASHRAE 189.1, Section 8.3.1.2.

For natural ventilation applications, provide monitoring to ensure that operable windows and other ventilation openings are operated appropriately to ensure adequate ventilation. This may include monitoring indoor and outdoor carbon dioxide levels and providing visual feedback to building operators and occupants.

EA 19.3 Apply Advanced Ventilation Approaches

Apply advanced ventilation approaches that have the potential to reduce energy use and improve IAQ, including the following methods:

- Dedicated outdoor air systems (DOAS)
- Demand-controlled ventilation
- Displacement ventilation
- Economizers
- Energy recovery ventilation
- Variable-air-volume systems

If any of these ventilation strategies are used, ASHRAE Standard 62.1 Ventilation Rate Procedure requirements must be met under all loads and occupancy conditions.

 See Appendix B: Communication and Education

ASSESSMENT PROTOCOLS (AP)	MINIMUM ACTIONS (MA)	EXPANDED ACTIONS (EA)
	MA 19.3 Meet ASHRAE Standard 62.1 for New Systems Design and install new HVAC systems to meet all requirements of ASHRAE Standard 62.1 using the Ventilation Rate Procedure. **Note** *ASHRAE Standard 62.1 also allows a Natural Ventilation Procedure in conjunction with mechanical ventilation systems, with a few specified exceptions. When natural ventilation is provided, efforts should be made to ensure windows and other ventilation openings are operated appropriately.* Ensure compliance with Section 5 of ASHRAE Standard 62.1. **MA 19.4 Code Precedent for Ventilation** If local codes require more ventilation than ASHRAE Standard 62.1 requirements, the local code requirements must be met.	**EA 19.4 Implement Pre-Occupancy Ventilation Control** For ventilation systems that serve spaces that are not continuously occupied, implement a control strategy to provide the design minimum outdoor air ventilation rate for a period of 1 hour prior to expected occupancy, whenever the spaces have been unventilated for a period longer than 24 hours.

References for Priority Issue 19.0 Outdoor Air Ventilation:

ASHRAE *Indoor Air Quality Guide*, Strategies 7.1 through 7.4, and 8.1 through 8.4
ASHRAE Standard 62.1, Sections 5 and 6
ASHRAE Standard 189.1, Section 8.3.1.2

ASSESSMENT PROTOCOLS (AP)	MINIMUM ACTIONS (MA)	EXPANDED ACTIONS (EA)

AP 20.1 Identify Localized Contaminant Sources That Require Exhaust Ventilation

Identify rooms or areas with localized contaminant sources, including the following:

- Kitchens
- Restrooms
- Locker rooms
- Vocational programs (e.g., welding, auto body, painting, printing, cosmetology)
- Soiled laundry storage rooms
- Art rooms and art storage areas
- Copy and printing rooms
- Areas where chemicals might be stored or used (e.g., janitor's closets)
- Spaces where contaminants are generated as part of processes, such as cooking and conducting scientific experiments
- Areas with high humidity (e.g., showers, bathtubs, cooking ranges, and commercial dishwashers)
- Attached parking garages

AP 20.2 Measure Airflow and Determine Compliance

Measure exhaust airflows on a room-by-room basis and determine whether the school complies with the exhaust requirements of ASHRAE Standard 62.1 for each space.

AP 20.3 Assess Exhaust Discharge Locations

Determine whether exhausts vent to the outdoors. Inspect or verify that exhaust from rooms with localized contaminant sources do not discharge or leak into other indoor spaces, ceiling plenums, parking garages, crawlspaces, attics or within walls.

MA 20.1 Provide Local Exhaust Where Needed and Meet ASHRAE Standard 62.1 Exhaust Rates

Ensure exhaust is provided for rooms or areas with localized indoor contaminant sources as identified in AP 20.1. If ASHRAE Standard 62.1 exhaust requirements are not met, repair, replace or install local exhaust ventilation to meet the requirements, ensuring that ducts are sized, installed and vented properly to the outdoors. Seal exhaust ductwork to improve performance and maintain negative pressure to reduce the potential for leakage into occupied spaces, plenums or other adjoining spaces as specified in ASHRAE Standard 62.1, Section 5.2. Measure and verify that exhaust airflows meet minimum requirements. Ensure sufficient make-up air for exhaust fans.

MA 20.2 Reduce Causes of Complaints Related to Inadequate Exhaust

If there are occupant complaints related to inadequate exhaust (e.g., odors, moisture), ensure that the following are operating properly:

- Mechanical equipment, ducts and combustion flues are in good condition. Ducts are not subject to corrosion, blockage or excessive leakage.
- There is no back draft from combustion flues under worst-case conditions.
- Exhaust fans are drawing air and the air is coming out of exhaust vents on the roof at the intended airflow rates.
- Exhaust draws contaminants away from, rather than toward, occupants.
- Exhausted room is under negative pressure relative to the surrounding spaces.
- Exhaust system is turned on, outdoor air grilles and air dampers are operating properly, and adequate make-up air is provided.
- Outdoor air dilutes contaminants from all sources. The ventilation system should provide sufficient outdoor air to all occupied spaces during all operating modes. See Priority Issue 19.0 Outdoor Air Ventilation.
- Airflow patterns provide proper air mixing.
- The exhaust system is not subject to excessive vibration.

EA 20.1 Prevent Recirculation of Exhausted Air

If exhaust recirculation is evident and if outdoor air intakes are located near exhaust vents and already satisfy minimum separation distance requirements, consider system changes that would further prevent recirculation of exhausted air.

EA 20.2 Monitor Exhaust Operation

If exhaust function is critical for safe operation, such as with welding hoods or paint spray booths in educational facilities, consider measuring stations and automatic alarms to indicate an operational failure and/ or failure to provide adequate exhaust air flows.

References for Priority Issue 20.0 Exhaust Ventilation:

ASHRAE *Indoor Air Quality Guide*, Strategy 6.3
ASHRAE Standard 62.1, Section 5, Section 6.5 and Table 6.5

 See Appendix B: Communication and Education

Safety

ASSESSMENT PROTOCOLS (AP)	MINIMUM ACTIONS (MA)	EXPANDED ACTIONS (EA)
AP 21.1 Assess School Building Safety Identify the school's health and safety representatives and include them in all building safety planning. Document safety hazards that were observed during the IAQ walkthrough, energy audit or other inspections. *Immediately respond to urgent and life-threatening situations.* Ensure that the results of the safety assessment are provided to the school's health and safety representatives and that corrective actions are considered as part of the building upgrades. **AP 21.2 Assess Fire Alarms, Smoke Alarms, and Carbon Monoxide Detection and Warning Equipment** Determine whether there are working fire alarms, smoke alarms, and carbon monoxide detection and warning equipment. Determine whether carbon monoxide detection and warning equipment meets the requirements of NFPA 720 and applicable local and state requirements. **AP 21.3 Identify Prevalence and Storage of Harmful Chemicals** Determine where harmful chemicals are located and whether the chemicals are stored correctly. Include custodial closets, storage areas under sinks, science laboratories, hospitality training programs, art laboratories, food laboratories and vocational programs (e.g., welding, auto body, painting, printing, cosmetology) during the assessment. Identify all storage locations for cleaning products and pesticides. If deficiencies are noted, see MA 21.3. **AP 21.4 Identify Risk of Mercury Exposure** Identify the extent to which mercury exposure is a risk in the building or a potential risk as part of the upgrade. Science classrooms and storerooms may contain supplies of elemental mercury or mercury compounds used as lab reagents and mercury-containing lab equipment, such as thermometers and barometers. Mercury may be used in other devices or equipment found in schools, such as fever thermometers and blood pressure measuring devices in nurse's offices, thermostats and fluorescent lighting. Determine whether the school has a mercury spill response plan.	**MA 21.1 Correct Safety Hazards Identified During the Assessments** *Immediately correct urgent and life-threatening safety risks.* Correct other safety hazards identified during the building upgrades. Provide education to staff and students on safety concerns. **MA 21.2 Correct Deficiencies With Fire Alarms, Smoke Alarms, and Carbon Monoxide Detection and Warning Equipment** Have qualified personnel correct deficiencies with fire alarms, smoke alarms, and carbon monoxide detection and warning equipment. If carbon monoxide detection and warning equipment is not present, install new equipment meeting the requirements of NFPA 720 and applicable local and state requirements. **MA 21.3 Ensure Appropriate Storage of Hazardous Chemicals** Recommend appropriate and controlled storage of hazardous chemicals and pesticides (e.g., remove from accessible locations). **MA 21.4 Prevent Mercury Exposure** Prepare a mercury spill response plan if none exists. Prevent mercury spills by removing all elemental mercury, mercury compounds and mercury-containing equipment (excluding fluorescent lighting and compact fluorescent light bulbs) and replacing them with non-mercury substitutes. Contact a qualified professional to collect and properly dispose of all elemental mercury supplies and mercury-containing devices and equipment. Properly dispose of fluorescent lighting, compact fluorescent light bulbs and mercury-containing thermostats that may be part of energy upgrade activities.	**EA 21.1 Install Enhanced Carbon Monoxide Detection and Warning Equipment** Install carbon monoxide detection and warning equipment capable of detecting and storing low peak carbon monoxide levels. Consider integrating carbon monoxide detection and warning equipment into the building's central monitoring system. Carbon monoxide detection and warning equipment must meet the requirements of NFPA 720 and applicable local and state requirements. **EA 21.2 Install Light Switches in Stairwells** Recommend installation of light switches at the top and bottom of all stairwells. **EA 21.3 Install Step Lighting** Consider installation of safety lighting on or near steps. Consider energy-efficient LED lighting. **EA 21.4 Repair Malfunctioning Doors, Windows, Roofs and Floors** Repair malfunctioning doors, windows, roofs and floors. **EA 21.5 Ensure Safety of Electrical Systems** Have qualified personnel ensure that electrical systems are in accordance with applicable codes.

 See Appendix B: Communication and Education   See Appendix C: Worker Protection

ASSESSMENT PROTOCOLS (AP)	MINIMUM ACTIONS (MA)	EXPANDED ACTIONS (EA)
AP 21.5 Identify Fire Extinguisher Locations Identify locations of fire extinguishers in the school and verify whether placement meets applicable laws. **AP 21.6 Assess Water Heater Temperatures** Determine whether the water heater temperature settings are within the allowable limits of the local and state codes.	**MA 21.5 Correct Fire Extinguisher Deficiencies** Ensure that fire extinguishers are placed according to applicable laws and correct as necessary. **MA 21.6 Adjust Water Heater Temperatures** Ensure that water heater set points do not exceed the allowable limits of local and state codes. Otherwise, ensure that water heater set points do not exceed 120 °F to prevent scalding.	

References for Priority Issue 21.0 Building Safety for Children and Other Occupants:

CDC-NIOSH Safety Checklist Program for Schools
EPA Chemical Management Resource Guide for School Administrators
EPA Compact Fluorescent Light Bulbs
EPA Healthy School Environments Assessment Tool (HealthySEAT)
EPA Mercury Releases and Spills
EPA Recycling Mercury-Containing Light Bulbs (Lamps)
EPA Toolkit for Safe Chemical Management in K–12 Schools
EPA Schools and Mercury
EPA Sensible Steps to Healthier School Environments
Minnesota Department of Health: Mercury Flooring Testing and Mitigation: Guidance for Environmental Professionals
Minnesota Pollution Control Agency: Disposal Guidance for Mercury-Catalyzed Polyurethane Flooring and Subflooring
NFPA 72: National Fire Alarm and Signaling Code
NFPA 720: Standard for the Installation of Carbon Monoxide (CO) Detection and Warning Equipment
Northeast Waste Management Officials' Association: Mercury Use in School Classrooms: Summary and Assessment of Non-Mercury Alternatives

ASSESSMENT PROTOCOLS (AP)	MINIMUM ACTIONS (MA)	EXPANDED ACTIONS (EA)
AP 22.1 Assess Occupancy During Construction Periods Determine the nature of building occupancy during construction periods. Identify the areas of the building that will be occupied. Identify any special needs of the building occupants (e.g., elderly faculty, young students, disabled students and faculty). Identify specific times of occupancy. Identify occupant complaints or concerns. **AP 22.2 Identify Contaminants and Pathways** Identify potential contaminant sources from building upgrades (e.g., activities, materials and equipment that have the potential to cause IAQ problems) and pathways through which contaminants could affect the air quality for the building occupants.	**MA 22.1 Minimize Children's and Other Occupants' Exposures During Upgrade Activities** When conducting activities that may result in exposure to airborne contaminants (e.g., cutting or grinding materials, painting, installing insulation) comply with local laws and adhere to the Sheet Metal and Air Conditioning Contractors' National Association's (SMACNA) Indoor Air Quality Guidelines for Occupied Buildings Under Construction. Minimize children's and other occupants' exposures to VOCs, particles or other airborne contaminants by the following procedures: • Restrict building occupants and workers without the personal protective equipment needed for the work being performed from the construction area. • Separate construction areas from occupied portions of the building using appropriate containment and ventilation practices. Ensure that work areas are properly isolated (e.g., by constructing a sealed, rigid-wall air barrier with a lockable door separating the work area from occupants or isolating smaller work areas with a plastic sheeting air barrier). Ensure that work areas are ventilated with exhaust to the outdoors to protect workers and occupants. Contaminants should be captured as close as possible to the source of the emissions. Work areas should be under a negative pressure relative to surrounding spaces. Ensure that exhausted construction contaminants do not re-enter the building. *Note* *If negative pressurization in the work areas is not possible, use an exhausted double wall buffer zone to separate work areas from surrounding areas.* • Ensure fire egress requirements from occupied portions of the building are maintained when isolating work areas. • Do not conduct dry-sanding without implementing containment measures for the dust generated. • Ensure sufficient ventilation and cure time of wet-applied materials to protect occupants before re-entry into work area. • Establish vehicle staging areas for loading and unloading materials and equipment at least 100 feet away from outdoor air intakes, operable windows and entryways to the building. • Clean the area thoroughly before re-entry of unprotected workers or occupants to ensure removal of any dusts that may contain pollutants. Use sealed, HEPA-rated vacuums. • Follow all manufacturers' printed instructions, which may indicate the need to evacuate building occupants and other unprotected individuals from work areas during and for some period after the use of a product. • Create specific plans to contain particulate matter during demolition activities. • Limit IAQ impact of airborne contaminants released by roofing materials during installation (e.g., hot mop asphalt, seam sealing on EPDM, polyvinyl chloride or modified bitumen roofing). Establish isolation barriers and keep roofing materials away from outdoor air intakes or conduct pollutant-generating roofing activities during unoccupied periods. • Promptly respond to any occupant complaints or concerns.	**EA 22.1 Consider and Implement Additional Protections As Appropriate** For situations that the assessment process classified as relatively high risk, consider implementing the following options: • Require rigid-wall air barriers with sealed, lockable entries between work areas and occupied spaces and provide negative pressurization to contain contaminants. • Create a buffer zone around work sites. • Restrict construction activities to off-hours when feasible. • Conduct temporary air cleaning. • Stage construction activities in controllable sizes. • Control pressurization and the indoor environment with temporary HVAC equipment. • Vacate the entire building, when feasible.

 See Appendix B: Communication and Education   See Appendix C: Worker Protection

MA 22.2 Protect HVAC Systems

Protect HVAC systems from contaminants during work activities.

- Seal openings in existing ducts located in work areas to avoid infiltration by dust and debris.

- New HVAC equipment, ducts, diffusers and return registers should be stored in a clean, dry place and should be covered to prevent dust accumulation.

- If operating an HVAC system that interfaces with the work areas, ensure that the system does not pull return air from the work area and install air filters with a MERV 8 rating or higher during construction activities.

- Visually inspect duct work after construction activities have been completed and clean internal surfaces as needed to remove dust and debris.

- Ensure that all filters used during work activities have been removed and that new filters are properly installed before operating the HVAC system during occupancy.

MA 22.3 Protect Highly Absorptive Materials

Protect any existing absorptive materials in place by fully covering with plastic sheeting. Fully secure all edges of the sheeting to protect materials from airborne contaminants and emissions caused by construction.

Schedule the installation of absorbent materials—such as ceiling tiles, fabrics, furnishings and carpet—after major dust and pollutant-generating activities are completed. Ensure that materials have not been exposed to moisture and are dry before installation.

MA 22.4 Safely Install Spray Foam Insulation

Employ safe work practices to avoid exposure to spray polyurethane foam (SPF). Follow the manufacturers' printed instructions for vacating building occupants and other unprotected individuals not involved in the application of the SPF products from the premises during and for some period after SPF application. Require and confirm SPF to be installed in strict accordance with manufacturer's requirements.

Note

The curing time (complete reaction) of SPF insulation varies depending on the type of product, application technique, temperature, humidity and other factors. While the SPF is curing it still contains unreacted chemicals, which include isocyanates and proprietary chemicals. Manufacturers estimate that it can take approximately 1 to 3 days after application for the two-component high pressure "professional" SPF system to fully cure and approximately 8 to 24 hours for the one-component foam to cure. Exposure to isocyanates may cause skin, eye and lung irritation, asthma, and sensitization. Exposures to isocyanates should be minimized. See EPA's Spray Polyurethane Foam *Web page for more information.*

References for Priority Issue 22.0 Protecting IAQ During Construction:

American Chemistry Council: Spray Polyurethane Foam Health and Safety
ASHRAE Standard 62.1, Section 7.1.4.2
ASHRAE Standard 189.1, Section 10.3.1.6
EPA *IAQ Tools for Schools,* IAQ Reference Guide, Section 3 – Effective Communication
EPA Spray Polyurethane Foam (SPF)
SMACNA IAQ Guidelines for Occupied Buildings Under Construction

	PRIORITY ISSUE 23.0 JOBSITE SAFETY

ASSESSMENT PROTOCOLS (AP)	MINIMUM ACTIONS (MA)	EXPANDED ACTIONS (EA)
AP 23.1 Evaluate Risks Evaluate existing and potential health concerns and activities. Refer to Appendix C: Worker Protection for recommended evaluation measures and actions.	**MA 23.1 Ensure Worker Protection** See Appendix C: Worker Protection for recommended actions to protect worker safety, including available resources.	This cell is intentionally blank.

 See Appendix C: Worker Protection

Abbreviations and Acronyms

AARST – American Association of Radon Scientists & Technologists, Inc.

ACCA – Air Conditioning Contractors of America

ACM – asbestos-containing material

AHERA – Asbestos Hazard Emergency Response Act

ANSI – American National Standards Institute

ASHRAE – American Society of Heating, Refrigerating and Air-Conditioning Engineers

ASTM – American Society for Testing and Materials

ATCM – Airborne Toxic Control Measures

CDC – Centers for Disease Control and Prevention

CFR – Code of Federal Regulations

DOAS – dedicated outdoor air system(s)

DOL – U.S. Department of Labor

EPA – U.S. Environmental Protection Agency

EPDM – ethylene propylene diene monomer

ft² – square feet

GPS – Green Performance Standards

HEPA – high-efficiency particulate air

HUD – U.S. Department of Housing and Urban Development

HVAC – Heating, Ventilation and Air Conditioning

HVAC&R – Heating, Ventilation, Air Conditioning and Refrigeration

IAQ – indoor air quality

IICRC – Institute of Inspection, Cleaning and Restoration Certification

IPM – integrated pest management

LED – light-emitting diode

MALB – Measurement for Schools and Large Buildings

MERV – minimum efficiency reporting value

NESHAP – National Emission Standards for Hazardous Air Pollutants

NFPA – National Fire Protection Association

NIOSH – National Institute for Occupational Safety and Health

NIST – National Institute of Standards and Technology

NVLAP – National Voluntary Laboratory Accreditation Program

OSHA – Occupational Safety and Health Administration

PCBs – polychlorinated biphenyls

pCi/L – picocuries per liter (in air)

PM – particulate matter

ppm – parts per million

RMS-LB – Radon Mitigation in Schools and Large Buildings

RRP – Renovation, Repair and Painting Program

SF Environment – San Francisco Department of the Environment

SMACNA – Sheet Metal and Air Conditioning Contractors' National Association

SPF – spray polyurethane foam

TSCA – Toxic Substances Control Act

UL – Underwriters Laboratories

VOC – volatile organic compound

ACCA (Air Conditioning Contractors of America) Standard 5 QI-2010: ANSI/ACCA Standard 5. HVAC Quality Installation Specification. 2010. http://www.acca.org/?smd_process_download=1&download_id=13274

ACCA Standard 6 QE-2007: ANSI/ACCA Standard 6. Restoring the Cleanliness of HVAC Systems. 2007. http://www.acca.org/?smd_process_download=1&download_id=13278

ACCA Standard 9 QIVP-2011: ANSI/ACCA Standard 9. HVAC Quality Installation Verification Protocols. 2011. http://www.acca.org/?smd_process_download=1&download_id=13286

American Academy of Pediatrics Committee on Environmental Health: Developmental toxicity: Special considerations based on age and developmental state. In Etzel, R., & S. Balk (Eds.), *Pediatric Environmental Health* (2nd Edition, pp. 9–36). Elk Grove Village, IL. 2003.

American Chemistry Council: Spray Polyurethane Foam Health and Safety. http://www.spraypolyurethane.org

American Transportation Research Institute: Compendium of Idling Regulations. 2012. http://www.atri-online.org/research/idling/ATRI_Idling_Compendium.pdf

ANSI (American National Standards Institute)/ AARST (American Association of Radon Scientists & Technologists, Inc.) MALB: Radon Measurement for Schools and Large Buildings. Under development, expected availability late 2014. See http://www.aarst.org/bookstore.shtml

ANSI/AARST RMS-LB: Radon Mitigation in Schools and Large Buildings. Under development, expected availability late 2014. See http://www.aarst.org/bookstore.shtml

ANSI/CSA (Canadian Standards Association) Z21 and Z83 Series: Products and Standards for Gas, Oil and Solid Fuel Appliances and Equipment. http://www.ul.com/global/fra/pages/offerings/industries/appliancesandhvac/gasoilsolidfuel/ansi/

ANSI Z21.11.2/CSA: ANSI Standard Z21.11.2-2013. Gas-Fired Room Heaters, Volume II, Unvented Room Heaters. 2013. http://webstore.ansi.org/RecordDetail.aspx?sku=ANSI+Z21.11.2-2013

ANSI Z223.1/NFPA (National Fire Protection Association) 54: ANSI Standard Z223.1/NFPA 54: National Fuel Gas Code. 2012. http://www.nfpa.org/catalog/product.asp?pid=5412&title=2012-NFPA-54-National-Fuel-Gas-Code&category_name=&target_pid=5412&source_pid=5409&link_type=edition_change

ASHRAE (American Society of Heating, Refrigerating and Air-Conditioning Engineers): *ASHRAE Fundamentals Handbook.* 2013. http://www.techstreet.com/ashrae/products/1858809

ASHRAE: *ASHRAE Handbook—HVAC Applications.* 2011. https://www.ashrae.org/resources--publications/Description-of-the-2011-ASHRAE-Handbook-HVAC-Applications

ASHRAE: *Humidity Control Design Guide for Commercial and Institutional Buildings.* 2001. http://www.techstreet.com/ashrae/products/1212230

ASHRAE: *Indoor Air Quality Guide: Best Practices for Design, Construction and Commissioning.* 2009. https://www.ashrae.org/resources--publications/bookstore/indoor-air-quality-guide.

ASHRAE: *Load Calculations Applications Manual.* 2009. http://www.techstreet.com/ashrae/products/1703600

ASHRAE: *Procedures for Commercial Building Energy Audits, 2nd Edition.* 2011. http://www.techstreet.com/ashrae/products/1809206

ASHRAE: *The ASHRAE Guide for Buildings in Hot and Humid Climates, 2nd Edition.* 2009. http://www.techstreet.com/products/1609865

ASHRAE Guideline 0-2013: The Commissioning Process. 2013. http://www.techstreet.com/ashrae/products/1870180

ASHRAE Guideline 1.1-2007: HVAC&R Technical Requirements for the Commissioning Process. 2007. http://www.techstreet.com/products/1573306

ASHRAE Standard 62.1: ANSI/ASHRAE Standard 62.1-2013. Ventilation for Acceptable Indoor Air Quality. 2013. http://www.techstreet.com/ashrae/products/1865968

ASHRAE Standard 180: ANSI/ACCA/ASHRAE Standard 180-2012. Standard Practice for Inspection and Maintenance of Commercial Building HVAC Systems. 2012. http://www.techstreet.com/ashrae/products/1832333

ASHRAE Standard 188P: ASHRAE Standard 188P (proposed). Legionellosis: Risk Management for Building Water Systems.

ASHRAE Standard 189.1: ANSI/ASHRAE Standard 189.1-2011. Standard for the Design of High-Performance Green Buildings: Except Low-Rise Residential Buildings. 2011. https://www.ashrae.org/resources--publications/bookstore/standard-189-1

Association of Physical Plant Administrators: Operational Guidelines for Educational Facilities: Custodial. Alexandria, VA. 2011. http://www.appa.org/bookstore/product_browse.cfm?itemnumber=691

ASTM International D6670: ASTM Standard D6670-13 (2013). Standard Practice for Full-Scale Chamber Determination of Volatile Organic Emissions from Indoor Materials/Products. 2013. http://www.astm.org/Standards/D6670.htm

ASTM International E2600: ASTM Standard E2600-10. Standard Guide for Vapor Encroachment Screening on Property Involved in Real Estate Transactions. 2010. http://www.astm.org/Standards/E2600.htm

ASTM International E2813: ASTM E281312. Standard Practice for Building Enclosure Commissioning. 2012. http://www.astm.org/Standards/E2813.htm

Borgeson, M., and Zimring, M.: Financing Energy Upgrades for K–12 School Districts: A Guide to Tapping Into Funding for Energy Efficiency and Renewable Energy Improvements. 2013. Lawrence Berkeley National Laboratory. Report LBNL-6133E. http://emp.lbl.gov/sites/all/files/lbnl-6133e.pdf

California Air Resources Board: Hazardous Ozone-Generating "Air Purifiers." 2012. California Environmental Protection Agency. http://www.arb.ca.gov/research/indoor/ozone.htm

California Department of Public Health, Emission Testing Method for California Specification 01350: Standard Method for the Testing and Evaluation of Volatile Organic Chemical Emissions From Indoor Sources Using Environmental Chambers, Version 1.1. 2010. http://www.cdph.ca.gov/programs/IAQ/Documents/cdph-iaq_standardmethod_v1_1_2010%20new1110.pdf

California Title 17: California Code of Regulations, Title 17. Sections 93120-92120.12. 2007. http://www.arb.ca.gov/regact/2007/compwood07/fro-final.pdf

Carpet and Rug Institute: Green Label/Green Label Plus. http://www.carpet-rug.org/CRI-Testing-Programs/Green-Label-Plus.aspx

CDC (Centers for Disease Control and Prevention): Asthma in the U.S. 2011. http://www.cdc.gov/vitalsigns/Asthma.

CDC: Guidelines for School Health Programs To Prevent Tobacco Use and Addiction. 1994. http://www.cdc.gov/mmwr/PDF/RR/RR4302.pdf

CDC: Rodents. 2010. http://www.cdc.gov/rodents

CDC, National Institute for Occupational Safety and Health (NIOSH): Dampness and Mold Assessment Tool. 2013. http://www.cdc.gov/niosh/topics/indoorenv/mold.html#8

CDC, NIOSH: Safety Checklist Program for Schools. 2003. http://www.cdc.gov/niosh/docs/2004-101/

Collaborative for High Performance Schools: Best Practices Manual, Volume V. Commissioning of High Performance Schools. 2006. http://www.chps.net/dev/Drupal/node/40

Collaborative for High Performance Schools: High Performance Products Database. http://www.chps.net/dev/Drupal/node/445

Consumer Product Safety Commission: FAQs: Lead in Paint (And Other Surface Coatings). http://www.cpsc.gov/en/business--manufacturing/business-education/lead/faqs-lead-in-paint-and-other-surface-coatings/

EPA (U.S. Environmental Protection Agency): Air and Radiation. National Ambient Air Quality Standards. 2012. http://www.epa.gov/air/criteria.html

EPA: Air Trends. 2013. http://www.epa.gov/airtrends/

EPA: AirNow. http://www.airnow.gov/

EPA: An Introduction to Indoor Air Quality (IAQ). Carbon Monoxide (CO). 2013. http://www.epa.gov/iaq/co.html

EPA: An Introduction to Indoor Air Quality (IAQ): Volatile Organic Compounds (VOCs). 2012. http://www.epa.gov/iaq/voc.html

EPA: Asbestos. Monitoring Asbestos-Containing Material (ACM). 2014. http://www2.epa.gov/asbestos/monitoring-asbestos-containing-material-acm

EPA: Asbestos NESHAP (National Emission Standards for Hazardous Air Pollutants). 2014. http://www2.epa.gov/asbestos/asbestos-neshap

EPA: Asbestos. State Asbestos Contacts. 2014. http://www2.epa.gov/asbestos/state-asbestos-contacts

EPA: Asbestos. School Buildings. 2014. http://www2.epa.gov/asbestos/school-buildings

EPA: Asbestos-Containing Materials in Schools. Final Rule and Notice (40 CFR Part 763). 1987. http://www.epa.gov/sbo/pdfs/fr-3269-8.pdf

EPA: Chemical Management Resource Guide for School Administrators. 2013. http://www.epa.gov/oppt/pubs/chemmgmt/

EPA: Clean School Bus—Idle Reduction Campaign. 2012. http://www.epa.gov/cleanschoolbus/antiidling.htm

EPA: Compact Fluorescent Light Bulbs (CFLs). 2014. http://www.epa.gov/cfl/

EPA: Drinking Water in Schools & Child Care Facilities. 2012. http://water.epa.gov/infrastructure/drinkingwater/schools/index.cfm

EPA: ENERGY STAR® Building Upgrade Manual. 2008. http://www.energystar.gov/ia/business/EPA_BUM_Full.pdf?77f4-4b9b

EPA: ENERGY STAR® Colorado Springs School District 11—Achieving Healthy Indoor Learning Environments Through Energy Efficiency Upgrades. 2008. http://www.energystar.gov/ia/business/k12_schools/ENERGY_STAR_Case_Study-Achieving_Healthy_Indoor_Environments_CG0807.pdf

EPA: Engineering Issue. Indoor Air Vapor Intrusion Mitigation Approaches. 2008. http://www.epa.gov/nrmrl/pubs/600r08115.html

EPA: Formaldehyde Emissions From Composite Wood Products. 2014. http://www.epa.gov/oppt/chemtest/formaldehyde/

EPA: Healthy School Environments Assessment Tool (HealthySEAT). 2011. http://www.epa.gov/schools/guidelinestools/healthySEAT

EPA: *IAQ Design Tools for Schools.* 2012. http://www.epa.gov/iaq/schooldesign/index.html

EPA: *IAQ Design Tools for Schools.* Commissioning. 2012. http://www.epa.gov/iaq/schooldesign/commissioning.html

EPA: *IAQ Design Tools for Schools.* Controlling Pollutants and Sources. 2013. http://www.epa.gov/iaq/schooldesign/controlling.html

EPA: *IAQ Design Tools for Schools.* Moisture Control. 2012. http://www.epa.gov/iaq/schooldesign/moisturecontrol.html

EPA: *IAQ Design Tools for Schools.* Preventing the Entry of Pollutants From Outside the Building. Entry Mat Barriers. 2013. http://www.epa.gov/iaq/schooldesign/controlling.html#Entry Mat Barriers

EPA: *IAQ Tools for Schools.* Action Kit. http://www.epa.gov/iaq/schools/actionkit.html

EPA: *IAQ Tools for Schools.* Action Kit: Background Information for Integrated Pest Management Checklist. http://www.epa.gov/iaq/schools/pdfs/kit/checklists/ipmcklstbkgd.pdf

EPA: *IAQ Tools for Schools.* Action Kit: Building and Grounds Maintenance Checklist. http://www.epa.gov/iaq/schools/pdfs/kit/checklists/bldgmaintchklst.pdf

EPA: *IAQ Tools for Schools.* Action Kit: Integrated Pest Management Checklist. http://www.epa.gov/iaq/schools/pdfs/kit/checklists/ipmcklst.pdf

EPA: *IAQ Tools for Schools.* Action Kit: Ventilation Checklist. http://www.epa.gov/iaq/schools/pdfs/kit/checklists/ventchklst.pdf

EPA: *IAQ Tools for Schools.* Action Kit: Walkthrough Inspection Checklist. http://www.epa.gov/iaq/schools/pdfs/kit/checklists/walkthruchklst.pdf

EPA: *IAQ Tools for Schools.* Develop Your Program, Key Drivers: Case Studies. 2012. http://epa.gov/iaq/schools/casestudies.html

EPA: *IAQ Tools for Schools.* IAQ Coordinator's Guide: A Guide to Implementing an IAQ Program. 2012. http://www.epa.gov/iaq/schools/tfs/guidtoc.html

EPA: *IAQ Tools for Schools.* IAQ Reference Guide. Appendix F: Secondhand Smoke. 2012. http://www.epa.gov/iaq/schools/tfs/guidef.html

EPA: *IAQ Tools for Schools.* IAQ Reference Guide. Appendix H: Mold and Moisture. 2012. http://www.epa.gov/iaq/schools/tfs/guideh.html

EPA: *IAQ Tools for Schools.* IAQ Reference Guide. Section 3: Effective Communication. 2012. http://www.epa.gov/iaq/schools/tfs/guide3.html

EPA: *IAQ Tools for Schools.* The *Indoor Air Quality Tools for Schools* Approach: Providing a Framework for Success. http://www.epa.gov/iaq/schools/pdfs/framework.pdf

EPA: Lead. Details on Certification Requirements for Firms. 2014. http://www2.epa.gov/lead/details-certification-requirements-firms

EPA: Lead. EPA Recognition of Lead Test Kits. 2014. http://www2.epa.gov/lead/epa-recognition-lead-test-kits

EPA: Lead. Locate Certified Inspection, Risk Assessment, and Abatement Firms. http://cfpub.epa.gov/flpp/search.cfm?Applicant_Type=firm

EPA: Lead. Renovation, Repair and Painting Program. 2014. http://www2.epa.gov/lead/renovation-repair-and-painting-program

EPA: Locate an RRP Training Class or Provider in Your Area. http://cfpub.epa.gov/flpp/searchrrp_training.htm

EPA: Mercury Releases and Spills. 2014. http://www.epa.gov/hg/spills/index.htm

EPA: Moisture Control Guidance for Building Design, Construction and Maintenance. 2013. http://www.epa.gov/iaq/pdfs/moisture-control.pdf

EPA: Mold and Moisture. Mold Remediation in Schools and Commercial Buildings. 2008. http://www.epa.gov/mold/mold_remediation.html

EPA: Ozone Generators That Are Sold as Air Cleaners. 2013. http://www.epa.gov/iaq/pubs/ozonegen.html

EPA: Pesticides. Integrated Pest Management (IPM) in Schools. 2014. http://www.epa.gov/opp00001/ipm/

EPA: *PestWise—Integrated Pest Management in Schools.* 2013. http://epa.gov/pesp/publications/ipm/ipm_in_schools_brochure.pdf

EPA: Polychlorinated Biphenyls (PCBs). 2014. http://www.epa.gov/epawaste/hazard/tsd/pcbs/index.htm

EPA: Polychlorinated Biphenyls (PCBs). Current Best Practices for PCBs in Caulk Fact Sheet—Interim Measures for Assessing Risk and Taking Action To Reduce Exposure. 2014. http://www.epa.gov/pcbsincaulk/caulkinterim.htm

EPA: Polychlorinated Biphenyls (PCBs). Fact Sheets for Schools and Teachers About PCB-Contaminated Caulk. 2012. http://www.epa.gov/pcbsincaulk/caulkschoolkit.htm

EPA: Polychlorinated Biphenyls (PCBs). PCB-Containing Fluorescent Light Ballasts (FLBs) in School Buildings: A Guide for School Administrators and Maintenance Personnel. 2013. http://www.epa.gov/osw/hazard/tsd/pcbs/pubs/ballasts.htm

EPA: Polychlorinated Biphenyls (PCBs). PCBs in Caulk in Older Buildings. 2014. http://www.epa.gov/pcbsincaulk

EPA: Polychlorinated Biphenyls (PCBs). Polychlorinated Biphenyls (PCBs) Manufacturing, Processing, Distribution in Commerce, And Use Prohibitions, 40 CFR Part 761 Subpart D—Storage and Disposal. 2007. http://www.gpo.gov/fdsys/pkg/CFR-2007-title40-vol30/pdf/CFR-2007-title40-vol30-part761.pdf

EPA: Polychlorinated Biphenyls (PCBs). Public Health Levels for PCBs in Indoor School Air. 2012. http://www.epa.gov/epawaste/hazard/tsd/pcbs/pubs/caulk/maxconcentrations.htm

EPA: Polychlorinated Biphenyls (PCBs). Regional PCB Coordinators. 2013. http://www.epa.gov/osw/hazard/tsd/pcbs/pubs/coordin.htm

EPA: Polychlorinated Biphenyls (PCBs). Steps to Safe Renovation and Abatement of Buildings That Have PCB-Containing Caulk. 2012. http://www.epa.gov/pcbsincaulk/guide/index.htm

EPA: Radon (Rn). Where You Live. 2013. http://www.epa.gov/radon/whereyoulive.html

EPA: Recycling Mercury-Containing Light Bulbs (Lamps). 2012. http://www.epa.gov/osw/hazard/wastetypes/universal/lamps/index.htm

EPA: Toolkit for Safe Chemical Management in K–12 Schools. 2012. http://www.epa.gov/schools/guidelinestools/toolkit.html

EPA: School Siting Guidelines. 2011. http://www.epa.gov/schools/guidelinestools/siting

EPA: Schools and Mercury. 2014. http://www.epa.gov/hg/schools.htm

EPA: Sensible Steps to Healthier School Environments. 2012. http://yosemite.epa.gov/R10/ecocomm.nsf/childrenshealth/sensible-steps-webinars

EPA: Small Entity Compliance Guide To Renovate Right: EPA's Lead-Based Paint Renovation, Repair, and Painting Program. 2011. http://www2.epa.gov/sites/production/files/documents/sbcomplianceguide.pdf

EPA: Spray Polyurethane Foam (SPF) Home. 2013. http://www.epa.gov/dfe/pubs/projects/spf/spray_polyurethane_foam.html

EPA: State School Environmental Health Guidelines. 2012. http://www.epa.gov/schools/guidelinestools/ehguide/

EPA: Vapor Intrusion. 2013. http://www.epa.gov/oswer/vaporintrusion/

EPA: Wastes, Hazardous Wastes, Test Methods, SW-846. 2013. http://www.epa.gov/waste/hazard/testmethods/sw846/index.htm

EPA, Office of Research and Development: A Decade of Children's Environmental Health Research: Highlights From EPA's Science To Achieve Results Program. 2007. EPA/600/S-07/038. http://epa.gov/ncer/publications/research_results_synthesis/ceh_report_508.pdf

EPA and CDC, NIOSH: Building Air Quality: A Guide for Building Owners and Facility Managers. 1991. http://www.epa.gov/iaq/largebldgs/pdf_files/iaq.pdf

Green Seal Standard GS-11: Green Seal™ Standard for Paints and Coatings. 3rd Edition. 2011. http://www.greenseal.org/Portals/0/Documents/Standards/GS-11/GS-11_Paints_and_Coatings_Standard.pdf

Greenguard Environmental Institute: Greenguard Gold. http://www.greenguard.org/en/manufacturers/manufacturer_childrenSchools.aspx

Haverinen-Shaughnessy, U., Moschandreas, D., and Shaughnessy, R.: Association between substandard classroom ventilation rates and students' academic achievement. 2011. *Indoor Air*, 21(2):121–31. http://onlinelibrary.wiley.com/doi/10.1111/j.1600-0668.2010.00686.x/full

Institute of Inspection, Cleaning and Restoration Certification: BSR-IICRC S520 Mold Remediation. Standard and Reference Guide for Professional Mold Remediation. 2008. http://www.iicrc.org/standards/iicrc-s520/

International Code Council: International Building Code. 2012. http://publiccodes.cyberregs.com/icod/ibc/2012/

Kats, G.: Greening America's Schools: Costs and Benefits. October 2006. A Capital E Report. http://www.usgbc.org/Docs/Archive/General/Docs2908.pdf

Landrigan, P., Schechter, C., Lipton, J., Fahs, M., and Schwartz, J.: Environmental pollutants and disease in American children: Estimates of morbidity, mortality, and costs for lead poisoning, asthma, cancer, and developmental disabilities. 2002. *Environmental Health Perspectives*, 110 (7):721–728. http://www.ncbi.nlm.nih.gov/pmc/articles/PMC1240919/pdf/ehp0110-000721.pdf

Lawrence Berkeley National Laboratory: Indoor Air Quality Scientific Findings Resource Bank. 2014. http://iaqscience.lbl.gov/sfrb.html

Master Painters Institute: MPI Green Vision. MPI Green Performance Standard/MPI Extreme Green. 2012. http://specifygreen.com/

Mendell, M., Eliseeva E., Davies, M., Spears, M., Lobsheid, A., Fisk, W., and Apte, M.: Association of classroom ventilation with reduced illness absence: A prospective study in California elementary schools. 2013. *Indoor Air* 23(6):515–28. http://onlinelibrary.wiley.com/doi/10.1111/ina.12042/full

Minnesota Department of Health: Mercury Flooring Testing and Mitigation. Guidance for Environmental Professionals. 2012. http://www.health.state.mn.us/divs/eh/hazardous/topics/mercury/hgflooringprofguide.html

Minnesota Pollution Control Agency: Disposal Guidance for Mercury-Catalyzed Polyurethane Flooring and Subflooring. 2008. http://www.pca.state.mn.us/index.php/view-document.html?gid=9065

National Institute of Building Sciences Whole Building Design Guide: Planning and Conducting Integrated Design (ID) Charrettes. 2013. http://www.wbdg.org/resources/charrettes.php

NFPA (National Fire Protection Association) 31: Standard for the Installation of Oil-Burning Equipment. 2011. http://www.nfpa.org/catalog/product.asp?pid=3111&cookie_test=1

NFPA 72: National Fire Alarm and Signaling Code. 2013. http://www.nfpa.org/codes-and-standards/document-information-pages?mode=code&code=72

NFPA 96: Standard for Ventilation Control and Fire Protection of Commercial Cooking Operations. 2014. http://www.nfpa.org/catalog/product.asp?pid=9614&title=&category_name=&target_pid=9614&source_pid=9611&link_type=edition_change

NFPA 211: Standard for Chimneys, Fireplaces, Vents and Solid Fuel-Burning Appliances. 2013. http://www.nfpa.org/catalog/product.asp?pid=21113&title=&category_name=&target_pid=21113&source_pid=21110&link_type=edition_change

NFPA 720: Standard for the Installation of Carbon Monoxide (CO) Detection and Warning Equipment. 2012. http://www.nfpa.org/catalog/product.asp?link_type=buy_box&pid=72012&icid=B484

NIST (National Institute of Standards and Technology)/NVLAP (National Voluntary Laboratory Accreditation Program): Directory of Accredited Laboratories. Asbestos Fiber Analysis (PLM Test Method). 2014. http://ts.nist.gov/Standards/scopes/plmtm.htm

NIST/NVLAP: Directory of Accredited Laboratories. Asbestos Fiber Analysis (TEM Test Method). 2014. http://ts.nist.gov/Standards/scopes/temtm.htm

Northeast Waste Management Officials' Association: Mercury Use in School Classrooms: Summary and Assessment of Non-Mercury Alternatives. 2007. http://www.newmoa.org/prevention/mercury/schools/MercuryAlternativesReport.pdf

OSHA (Occupational Safety and Health Administration), 29 CFR Part 1926.1101: Asbestos. Safety and Health Regulations for Construction: Toxic and Hazardous Substances. http://www.osha.gov/pls/oshaweb/owadisp.show_document?p_id=10862&p_table=STANDARDS

OSHA: Asbestos. http://www.osha.gov/SLTC/asbestos/

OSHA: Asbestos. Construction. http://www.osha.gov/SLTC/asbestos/construction.html

OSHA: Lead. http://www.osha.gov/SLTC/lead/

OSHA: Technical Manual, Section III, Chapter 7. Legionnaires' Disease. 1999. http://www.osha.gov/dts/osta/otm/otm_iii/otm_iii_7.html

Resilient Floor Covering Institute: FloorScore. http://www.rfci.com/

San Francisco Department of the Environment: Pest Prevention by Design Guidelines. 2012. http://www. sfenvironment.org/download/pest-prevention-by-design-guidelines

Scientific Certification Systems: SCS-EC-10.2-2007. Environmental Certification Program: Indoor Air Quality Performance. 2007. http://www.scscertified.com/docs/SCS-EC10.2-2007.pdf

Sheet Metal and Air-Conditioning Contractors' National Association: IAQ Guidelines for Occupied Buildings Under Construction, Second Edition. 2007. ANSI/SMACNA 008-2008. http://smacna.org/store

Toxic Substances Control Act Title VI: Formaldehyde Standards for Composite Wood Products. 2010. http://www.gpo.gov/fdsys/pkg/BILLS-111s1660enr/pdf/BILLS-111s1660enr.pdf

U.S. Code, Title 20, Chapter 68, Section 6083: Nonsmoking policy for children's services. 2012. http://www.gpo.gov/fdsys/granule/USCODE-2011-title20/USCODE-2011-title20-chap68-subchapX-partB-sec6083/content-detail.html

U.S. Department of Agriculture: Cooperative Extension System Offices. 2014. http://www.csrees.usda.gov/Extension/

U.S. Department of Housing and Urban Development: Lead Safe Work Practices. http://www.hud.gov/offices/cpd/affordablehousing/training/web/leadsafe/keyrequirements/safepractices.cfm

Wargocki, P., and Wyon, D.: Research Report: Effects of HVAC on student performance. October 2006. *ASHRAE Journal*, 22–28. http://www.techstreet.com/products/1719013

Section 3

Appendices

The core technical component of **Energy Savings Plus Health: Indoor Air Quailty Guidelines for School Building Upgrades** is **Section 2: Assessment Protocols and Recommended Actions**, which references the following appendices provided in this section:

Appendix A: Project Planning and Developing a Project Team

Appendix B: Communication and Education

Appendix C: Worker Protection

The appendices can be used to assist with project planning and the development of a project team, supplement the information in the assessment protocols and recommended minimum and expanded actions, provide communication and education strategies, and assist with worker protection. At the end of this section are lists of abbreviations and references cited in the appendices.

Project Planning

There are key steps during the building upgrade process that can provide opportunities to reduce costs and leverage synergies or, if not addressed adequately, can increase costs and lead to future challenges. These steps are outlined in **Table A1:**

Project Planning, and are detailed in **Section 2: Assessment Protocols and Recommended Actions** of the **Energy Savings Plus Health Guide**. These key planning steps can dramatically influence a project's direction, cost and outcomes and help maximize the impact of the Guide to help ensure a smooth project delivery.

Table A1: Project Planning

Table A1: Project Planning	
Integrated Design	Collaboration during building improvement projects can allow teams to solve problems creatively and with better outcomes for the building and for occupants than the traditional design and construction process.
	In an integrated process, project teams define the goals from the earliest stages of the project planning and carry these goals through to building occupancy and the operations and maintenance phases. Early engagement of all responsible parties avoids problems that occur when IAQ is treated as an afterthought and allows for consideration of alternative design concepts that improve IAQ and energy performance. Include an integrated design approach in the contract requirements for all design, construction and commissioning teams.
	Refer to Priority Issue 1.0 Project Planning/Integrated Design for more information.
Develop a Project Team	Create a strong project team that is committed to protecting IAQ throughout all phases of the project, from pre-design through building occupancy and use. Establishing a multidisciplinary team at the beginning is important to reduce design errors and provide opportunities for collaboration. A collaborative team will save the project time and money, as well as ensuring that energy consumption and IAQ goals are addressed from the beginning.
	Schedule regular full-team meetings to review design goals and collaboratively discuss challenges. Ensure that a school representative is always present during project meetings to ensure the overall project goals are guiding factors in discussion and to answer any operations and maintenance questions of the project team.
	Refer to Table A2: Developing a Project Team for more details.
Conceptualize the Project	As outlined in the Introduction of this Guide, IAQ is a critical component of school building upgrades because air quality can seriously affect the health of building occupants, especially children. During each energy upgrade or building renovation project, consider ways IAQ can be improved and ways that the upgrades under consideration could positively or negatively affect IAQ.

Table A1: Project Planning (continued)

Table A1: Project Planning	
Complete Energy and IAQ Audits	An energy audit identifies ways to improve energy efficiency in a building. An IAQ audit, sometimes referred to as an IAQ walkthrough inspection, identifies IAQ issues in a building that affect occupant health and safety. Sometimes, when equipment upgrades or operational changes are completed to improve energy efficiency, IAQ can be negatively affected. For example, performing energy upgrade activities without considering building ventilation can lead to decreased air quality, condensation problems, or elevated humidity levels that can cause mold growth. The resulting tradeoff for reduced operating cost from energy savings is decreased occupant health and safety. By performing both energy and IAQ audits and including IAQ planning in energy improvement projects, these potential negative effects can be mitigated while also taking advantage of the synergies of energy efficiency and IAQ. When planning for energy and IAQ audits, ask whether the energy auditor can assist an IAQ professional, such as the school's IAQ coordinator, with an IAQ assessment. Additionally, ask the energy auditor whether the outdoor ventilation rates are sufficient and if the controls are functioning properly, as ventilation plays a large role in both energy efficiency and IAQ. *Refer to AP 1.2 for more information on IAQ walkthroughs. Any final decisions regarding the project scope and plan should be made after the walkthrough and should ensure that major IAQ issues are accounted for and addressed.*
Identify Hazardous Materials	Hazardous materials such as lead, polychlorinated biphenyls (PCBs), asbestos and mold all pose significant health and safety issues to building occupants in old or even previously renovated buildings. These materials must be identified prior to starting work to ensure safe construction practices are used and that the materials are safely removed from the building as necessary. Removing these hazardous materials can be expensive, and any associated costs should be built into the project budget during the initial planning stages. *Refer to the following Priority Issues for specific information regarding potential locations of these materials within the building and for remediation guidance:* *3.0 Moisture Control and Mold* *4.0 Asbestos* *5.0 Lead* *6.0 Polychlorinated Biphenyls (PCBs)*
Test for Radon	Radon is a cancer-causing radioactive gas. It is odorless, colorless and tasteless, and it is a serious health and safety issue that must be addressed early in project planning. Measuring radon levels in schools is a relatively easy and straightforward process compared to many other important building upkeep activities. Mitigation of elevated radon levels can be more expensive, and any associated costs should be built into the project budget during the initial planning stages. *Refer to Priority Issue 7.0 Radon for testing and mitigation guidance.*
Design Charrette	Overall project goals, scope and systems-level strategy should be discussed during the Design Charrette or planning meeting. During this meeting, designers, engineers, and school representatives and decision makers should discuss strategy and synergies between IAQ and energy efficiency that can be implemented to achieve overall project goals. The Charrette should be concluded by outlining a defined project strategy. This strategy may include some "wish list" items that may later be ruled out based on cost; however, the goal of this meeting is to strategize tangible methods to achieve a school's desires so that the facility manager and other school decision makers can make informed final decisions about project scope. *Refer to MA 1.1 for more information on the Design Charrette process.*

Table A1: Project Planning	
Owner's Project Requirements (OPR)	The OPR is a formalized document that describes the school "owner's" project goals and functional requirements for how a building is designed and built. The OPR is a key document because design and construction teams will refer to it to ensure that project requirements and goals are achieved by design and construction decisions. In addition to the project design and construction team, the Commissioning Agent also will use the OPR as a foundation for the commissioning process, which also makes it integral to the quality assurance process. *Refer to MA 2.2 for more guidance and reference documents regarding the OPR.*
Commissioning Design Review/Quality Assurance During Design	Quality assurance checks are important to conduct during any building improvement project. Often, quality assurance is completed through the commissioning process. Although small improvement projects (e.g., minor system upgrades) may not warrant the cost of a full commissioning process completed by an outside firm, large multisystem projects (or projects providing improvements throughout the building) can achieve great value from following a formalized commissioning process. For these projects, a commissioning agent should be hired during the project's design phase, and the agent should see the project through to completion to ensure that all systems operate and function according to their design intent and/or optimum performance level. For small improvement projects, the system design and installation should at least be reviewed by a competent party, such as a facility manager or a building engineer. If a commissioning agent is hired, include contract requirements for at least one design review, including drawings and specifications, to ensure that quality assurance and commissioning considerations are implemented during design. For small projects, the facility manager or other qualified, unbiased party should perform this review. *Refer to MA 2.4 for more information on creating a commissioning plan.*
Construction Kick-Off Meeting	Prior to construction, conduct a kick-off meeting with the full team to discuss the OPR and all applicable Priority Issues that will need to be considered for the project. Unifying the project team prior to construction ensures that all team members have the same understanding of project goals, requirements, priorities and expectations.
Construction Planning: **Protecting Occupied Areas From Construction Pollutants**	If parts of the building will be occupied during the improvement project, ensure that the areas under construction are isolated with appropriate pressure control to limit construction dust and other pollutants from impacting occupants. Even small improvement activities, such as wall penetrations and touch-up painting, can generate indoor pollutants that lead to IAQ issues and health concerns. Before beginning any demolition or improvement project, create a plan to minimize contaminants from entering occupied buildings. *Refer to Priority Issue 22.0 Protecting IAQ During Construction. Additionally, refer to Appendix B: Communication and Education, which includes information to communicate with occupants to promote safety during construction.*
Retro-Commissioning	Retro-commissioning is a process of restoring existing systems to operate in accordance with their design intent and/or at the highest performance level possible. Generally, retro-commissioning focuses on energy-related systems, such as adjusting HVAC equipment and thermostat set points, adjusting direct digital controls and/or building automation systems, reprogramming automatic lighting controls, realigning daylight or occupancy sensors, rebalancing refrigerant levels, and recalibrating ventilation levels in each room. Repairing any operational issues and fine-tuning system functionality will improve IAQ and occupant comfort, as well as energy and resource efficiency. The need for retro-commissioning will be identified during a building energy audit, and retro-commissioning activities can be performed by an experienced commissioning agent. *For more information on building energy audits and retro-commissioning, refer to Priority Issue 2.0 Commissioning.*
Implementing Jobsite Safety	Assessing and implementing jobsite safety is important to protect visitors to the site and those performing work on the building. To minimize exposure to health and safety risks on the jobsite, see Appendix C: Worker Protection.

Table A1: Project Planning (continued)

Table A1: Project Planning	
Testing and Balancing and Onsite Commissioning	On completion of building construction and systems installations, onsite commissioning takes place to test, verify and fine-tune the performance of the newly installed systems. Onsite commissioning typically takes from one to several days. Often, the commissioning agent conducting the tests will find installation issues to address. Make sure to work with the commissioning agent to build time and resources into the project schedule for onsite commissioning and for addressing any issues found by the commissioning agent's inspection.
	Fixing systems outlined in the commissioning agent's issues log can delay projects, but taking action to fix any problems prior to occupancy will improve cost-effectiveness, reliability and long-term performance.
Building Flush-Out	To flush out all workspaces properly with outdoor air prior to occupancy, build additional time into the project completion schedule. The total recommended flush-out time varies depending on the project size and often ranges from 2 weeks to a full month to complete. Some period of flush-out time is better than none.
	Refer to MA 13.4 and EA 13.4 for more information.
Project Turnover and Systems Training	Working with a commissioning agent from the early planning phases can help to ensure that the building operates at the highest possible level of energy performance while meeting IAQ goals. In the commissioning agent's contract, require the development of comprehensive operations and maintenance training and systems manuals so that building operations and maintenance staff can keep the building functioning at the highest performance level.
	Refer to MA 2.8 and EA 2.3 for more information.
Solicit Continuous Feedback	Building occupants (e.g., school administrators, building planning management teams, teachers, health and safety staff, custodial staff, and students) are a great resource for identifying IAQ and energy efficiency concerns because they use and work in the building every day. These activities can promote occupant satisfaction in the long term:
	• Educate building occupants about the types of issues that could affect IAQ.
	• Create a clear process for building occupants to submit feedback and concerns.
	• Encourage schools to implement EPA's "*IAQ Tools for Schools*" program actions, if they are not already doing so.
	See Appendix B: Communication and Education.

Developing a Project Team

An integrated design approach is a drastic change from traditional design and construction practices. Traditionally, each discipline—such as the architect; mechanical, electrical, plumbing and civil engineers; and the construction team—would work independently. During planning and design, the architect often would lead the work by creating the overall building layout and then pass the design on to the engineers, who would all work independently. This type of process can create major design errors that go unchecked until the construction team tries to implement the design. A traditionally organized design team does not necessarily have a meeting with the construction team to review the project goals. Even if the design team understands that energy efficiency is extremely important to the school, this information may not be relayed to the construction team, which may make installation or purchasing decisions that it thinks are equivalent to the design but in the end do not meet the project's goals. **Table A2: Developing a Project Team** outlines who should be involved during each phase of the project to maximize collaboration, reduce the potential for misunderstandings and meet the goals of the project, which first and foremost prioritizes a healthy and productive indoor environment for children, teachers and all who use the school building.

Table A2: Developing a Project Team

Project/Phase	Key Personnel	Objectives
Project Identification (Goals and Scope)	Facility manager or school representative Building Planning Management Teams School faculty, staff, other stakeholders (e.g., parents and students, if possible) School IAQ coordinator, risk manager, and other IAQ team members Energy Auditor or Contractor	Identify energy efficiency improvement measures, energy impacts and IAQ synergies and challenges.
Project Planning and Design	Facility manager or school representative Building Planning Management Teams School faculty, staff, other stakeholders (e.g., parents and students, if possible) School IAQ coordinator, risk manager, and other IAQ team members Design Team, for example— • Architect • Interior designer • Mechanical engineer • Electrical engineer Commissioning agent or experienced school staff	Prepare for integrated design by including all design professionals in the planning process. Ensure that school representatives, such as the facility manager and interested faculty or staff members, are present at design meetings to ensure that the design meets the project goals. Designate the facility manager or a third-party commissioning agent to review proposed design for quality control.
Construction Permitting	Plan inspector, fire authority, etc.	Ensure that appropriate permits are obtained and that the design meets all applicable building codes.
Construction	General contractor Subcontractors Facility manager or school representative School IAQ coordinator, risk manager, and other IAQ team members Design professionals	Coordinate with contractor(s) to ensure that design and specifications are understood throughout the construction process and that IAQ goals are achieved. Provide opportunities for design professionals, contractors and school occupants to communicate IAQ concerns in a timely manner during construction.
Building Code Inspections	Code compliance officials (per project jurisdiction)	Ensure that the construction project meets all applicable building code requirements.

Table A2: Developing a Project Team (continued)

Table A2: Developing a Project Team		
Commissioning	Commissioning agent or experienced school staff Design Team, for example— • Architect • Interior designer • Mechanical engineer • Electrical engineer Facility manager or school representative School IAQ coordinator, risk manager, and other IAQ team members General contractor Subcontractors	The onsite inspection should be performed by a commissioning agent or other, experienced, responsible party to ensure that construction meets design requirements and all systems are operating properly.
Occupancy Turnover	Facility manager Facility maintenance staff Custodial staff School faculty, staff, other stakeholders (e.g., parents and students, if possible) School IAQ coordinator, risk manager, and other IAQ team members General contractor Subcontractors Manufacturer representatives	Train maintenance and custodial staff on required operation and maintenance procedures for new building systems. Highlight the potential for system failures and the IAQ effects of systems that are not operated properly.
Maintenance and Operation	Facility manager Facility maintenance staff Custodial staff School faculty, staff, other stakeholders (e.g., parents and students, if possible) School IAQ coordinator, risk manager, and other IAQ team members	Integrate required maintenance into the schedule for the facility. Provide opportunities for regular occupant feedback on IAQ concerns.

Renovation and construction projects in a school create unique challenges that affect the design and construction processes and the occupancy phase after work is complete. This appendix provides strategies for effective, proactive and responsive communications to help maintain a healthy and productive school indoor environment before, during and after a building upgrade.

It also is vital to ensure staff receive adequate training on operations, maintenance and repair after energy retrofits and building upgrades. Providing education to school faculty, staff and students about the IAQ goals of each project and information related to proper operation and occupancy can help to ensure that the renovated building and its systems continue to work as intended. This education reduces costs and risks to the overall project and the design and renovation/construction teams. This appendix outlines information about the project that should be provided to school facility managers, staff and students.

Effective Communications

Effective communications can help to prevent IAQ problems and allay unnecessary fears. In addition, schools should respond promptly and effectively to any IAQ issues that may arise. Effective, proactive and responsive communications are a critical, ongoing process for maintaining IAQ in the school. Communication can help school occupants understand how their activities affect IAQ, which will enable them to improve their indoor environment through proper choices and actions.

Proactive Communication

Schools and school districts can reap many benefits from taking a proactive approach to addressing IAQ issues. The positive public relations that can result from this approach can lead to a better understanding of IAQ by school occupants and the community. Communicating effectively, both internally and externally, is a key element.

Build rapport with the local media now. An informed media aware of your efforts to prevent IAQ problems and that understands the basics of IAQ in schools can be an asset instead of a liability during an IAQ crisis.

Communicating the goals of the IAQ Management Plan to those within the school—teachers, custodians, administrators, support staff, the school nurse, students—is key. The following steps can help develop good communication between you and the school occupants:

1. Provide accurate information about factors that are affecting IAQ.
2. Clarify the responsibilities and activities of the IAQ coordinator.
3. Clarify the responsibilities and activities of each occupant.
4. Notify occupants and parents of planned activities that may affect IAQ.
5. Employ good listening skills.

The necessary level of communication often depends on the severity of the IAQ complaint. If the complaint can be resolved quickly (e.g., an annoying but harmless odor from an easily identified source) and involves a small number of people, communication can be handled in a straightforward manner without risking confusion and bad feelings among school occupants. Communication becomes a more critical issue when there are delays in identifying and resolving the problem and when serious health concerns are involved.

Step 4 deals with informing occupants and parents before the start of significant planned activities that produce odors or contaminants. If occupants and parents are uninformed, they may become concerned about unknown air contaminants, such as strange odors or excessive levels of dust, and register an IAQ complaint. Examples of planned activities include pest control, painting, roofing and installation of new flooring. Notification of planned activities also can prevent problems from arising with students and staff with special needs. For example, an asthmatic student may wish to avoid certain areas within a school, or use alternative classrooms, during times when a major renovation project will produce higher levels of dust. A sample notification letter is provided in the model painting policy on the *EPA IAQ Tools for Schools* website.

Step 5 involves effective listening. School occupants often can provide information that helps prevent problems, and being "heard" may help defuse negative reactions by occupants if indoor air problems develop.

Responsive Communication

When an IAQ problem occurs, you can be assured that the school community will learn about it quickly. Without open communication, any IAQ problem can become complicated by anxiety, frustration and distrust. These complications can increase both the time and money needed to resolve the problem.

Immediate communication is vital and is easiest if a few strategic steps are taken before an IAQ problem arises. First, ensure that a spokesperson is ready by having a working understanding of the communication guidance found in this section and a background knowledge of IAQ as outlined in EPA's *IAQ Tools for Schools* IAQ Reference Guide. This person should also have complete access to information as the investigation progresses. Because of these qualifications, the school's IAQ coordinator may be a good choice for spokesperson. Second, establish a plan for how you will communicate to the school community. The school community includes all occupants of the school, parents, the school district administration and school board, the local union, and the local news media.

Paying attention to communication when solving a problem helps to ensure the support and cooperation of school occupants as the problem is investigated and resolved. There are basic, yet important, messages to convey:

- School administrators are committed to providing a healthy and safe school.
- Good IAQ is an essential component of a healthy indoor environment.
- IAQ complaints are taken seriously.

When a problem arises, communication should begin immediately. You should not wait until an investigation is nearly completed or until final data are available before providing some basic elements of information. Communications, whether in conversations or in writing, should include the following elements in a factual and concise manner:

- The general nature of the problem, the types of complaints that have been received, and the locations that are affected;

- The administration's policy in regard to providing a healthy and safe environment;
- What has been done to address the problems or complaints, including the types of information that are being gathered;
- What is currently being done, including factors that have been evaluated and found not to be causing or contributing to the problem;
- How the school community can help;
- Attempts that are being made to improve IAQ;
- Work that remains to be done and the expected schedule for its completion;
- The name and telephone number of the IAQ coordinator, who can be contacted for further information or to register complaints; and
- When the school will provide the next update.

Productive relations will be enhanced if the school community is given basic progress reports during the process of diagnosing and solving problems. It is advisable to explain the nature of investigative activities, so that rumors and suspicions can be countered with factual information. Notices or memoranda can be posted in general use areas and delivered directly to parents, the school board, the local union, and other interested constituents of the school community. Newsletter articles, the school website or other established communication channels also can be used to keep the school community up to date.

Problems can arise from saying either too little or too much. Premature release of information when data-gathering still is incomplete can cause confusion, frustration and future mistrust. Similar problems can result from incorrect representation of risk—improperly assuming the worst case or the best. If even simple

BEFORE PROBLEM | DURING PROBLEM

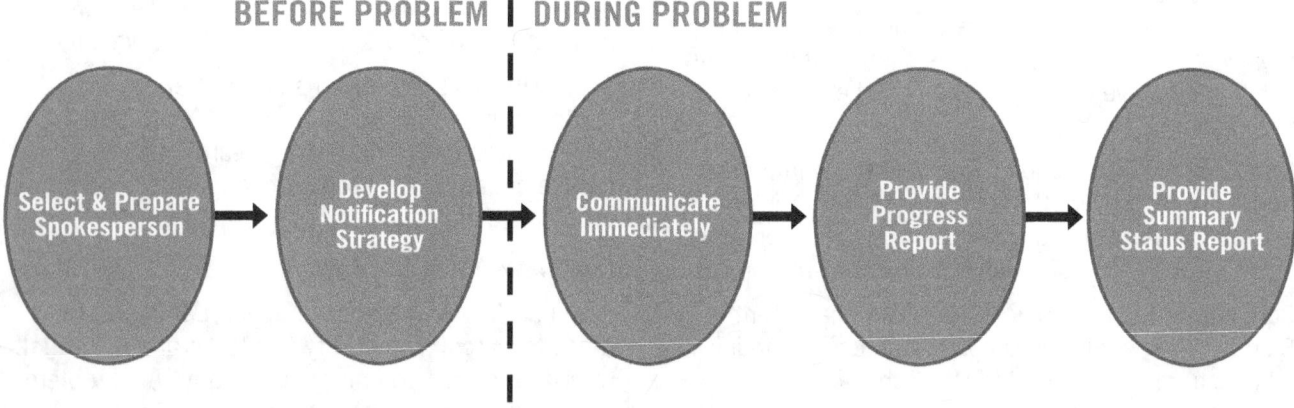

Select & Prepare Spokesperson → Develop Notification Strategy → Communicate Immediately → Provide Progress Report → Provide Summary Status Report

progress reports are not given, however, people will think either that nothing is being done or that something terrible is happening.

Even after the problem is correctly diagnosed and a proper mitigation strategy is in place, it may take days or weeks for contaminants to dissipate and symptoms to disappear. If building occupants are informed that their symptoms may persist for some time after solving the problem, the inability to bring instant relief is less likely to be seen as a failure.

Remember to communicate after problem-solving; although you may know that the problem has been resolved, the school community may not know, so be sure to provide a summary status report. The figure below summarizes the main steps for responsive communications.

Communication Principles

- *Be honest, frank and open.* Once trust and credibility are lost, they are almost impossible to regain. If you do not know an answer or are uncertain, say so. Admit mistakes. Get back to people with answers. Discuss data uncertainties, strengths and weaknesses.

- *Respect your audience.* Keep explanations simple, avoiding technical language and jargon as much as possible. Use concrete images that communicate on a personal level. People in the community often are more concerned about such issues as credibility, competence, fairness and compassion than about statistics and details; however, provide sufficient information to audiences that are capable of understanding more technical explanations.

- *Employ your best listening skills.* Take time to find out what people are thinking, rather than assuming that you already know.

- *Tailor communication strategies to your audience.* Use mass media for providing information and interpersonal techniques for changing attitudes.

- *Involve school employees.* An informed staff is likely to be a supportive staff.

- *Involve parents.* Inform parents about what is being done and why, as well as what will happen if problems are detected.

- *Involve the school board.* Encourage board members to observe the process (e.g., taking a walk through the school with the IAQ coordinator).

- *Involve businesses that provide services* to the school (e.g., exterminators, bus fleet administrators/operators) and businesses located around the school, which may also negatively affect IAQ.

- *Emphasize action.* Always try to include a discussion of actions that are underway or that can be taken.

- *Encourage feedback.* Accentuate the positive and learn from your mistakes.

- *Strive for an informed public.* The goal is for the public to be involved, interested, reasonable, thoughtful, solution-oriented and collaborative.

- *Be prepared for questions.* Provide background material on complex issues. Avoid public conflicts or disagreements among credible sources.

- *Be responsive.* Acknowledge the emotions that people express and respond in words and actions. When in doubt, lean toward sharing more information, not less, or people may think you are hiding something.

- *Combat rumors with facts.* For example, set up a chalkboard in the teachers' lounge or in another general use area for recording what is heard. Record rumors as they arise and add responses. Then pass out copies to the staff.

- *Do not overpromise.* Promise only what you can do and follow through with each promise.

- *Work with the media.* Be accessible to reporters and respect deadlines. Try to establish long-term relationships of trust with editors and reporters. Remember that the media are frequently more interested in politics than in science, more interested in simplicity than complexity, and more interested in danger than safety.

Priority IAQ Concerns and IAQ Considerations After the Building Upgrade

This section is organized by IAQ concerns (e.g., moisture control, asbestos, lead), in the same order as in the Assessment Protocols and Recommended Actions of Section 2 of this Energy Savings Plus Health Guide. Each IAQ concern is broken down into two columns:

- **Health Effects and Potential Exposure Locations:** This column explains how each IAQ concern can negatively affect health and identifies common locations within schools where the priority IAQ concern may be found. It also points to the appropriate Priority Issue(s) for further reading.

- **IAQ Considerations After the Building Upgrade:** A critical part of the education process occurs during building turnover, when facility managers and staff are trained in how to properly operate the new building and its systems. This column provides educational information for facility managers and staff on IAQ concerns to inspect for regularly, system and building operations reminders to promote healthy IAQ through operational practices, and opportunities to engage and educate other school occupants about protecting IAQ.

The following icon is used in Appendix B:

 Indicates an opportunity to communicate important messages via a sign or placard in the building.

Priority IAQ Concern	Health Effects and Potential Exposure Locations	IAQ Considerations After the Building Upgrade
Moisture Control and Mold	**Health Effects** Mold exposure can both cause and exacerbate respiratory-related health issues, such as allergic reactions and asthma. **Potential Exposure Locations** Mold can grow in any area with long-term moisture exposure, including exposure from large spills, equipment overflows or plumbing leaks; leakage through roofs, windows or openings in the building envelope; seepage from improperly sloped sites; or spaces with high humidity, such as locker rooms, crawlspaces and basement storage areas. **Further Reading** Priority Issue 3.0 Moisture Control and Mold	**Regular Inspections** School staff should regularly inspect bathrooms, locker rooms, science laboratories and other rooms with high humidity levels or potential for condensation or plumbing leaks. **System and Building Operations** Operate the HVAC system and use additional dehumidification if necessary to keep relative humidity levels below 60%, ideally between 30% and 50%, if possible. Relative humidity levels above 60% can create an environment conducive to mold growth. Indoor air can become too dry for occupant comfort and health during the heating season, particularly in northern and high-altitude locations. Ensure the regularly scheduled maintenance of humidification equipment and controls installed to maintain a low relative humidity limit (e.g., 30%). Improperly maintained humidification equipment can lead to microbiological problems. **Administrator and Staff Education** The EPA course "Introduction to Mold and Mold Remediation for Environmental and Public Health Professionals" provides an overview of mold prevention and mold remediation. It is based on EPA's voluntary guidance document "Mold Remediation in Schools and Commercial Buildings." Public health and environmental health professionals who are involved with mold issues may be interested in this course. Building managers, custodians, remediators, contractors and other professionals who respond to mold problems also may want to refer to this course. **Occupant Feedback** Ensure that school administrators, staff and students know whom to notify if they see spills, leaks, condensation, or other signs of standing moisture or moisture damage. Complaints of musty odors also may indicate moisture or condensation issues and should be investigated. **Student Education Opportunities for Teachers** Teach students about the link between mold and moisture and the associated health risks. See EPA's Teacher Resources and Lesson Plans website for a link to the educational material, "Hold the Mold."

Priority IAQ Concern	Health Effects and Potential Exposure Locations	IAQ Considerations After the Building Upgrade
Asbestos	**Health Effects** Exposure to asbestos can cause lung cancer, mesothelioma (cancer of the lining of the chest and abdominal cavity) and asbestosis, in which the lungs become scarred with fibrous tissue.[a] **Potential Exposure Locations** Asbestos is a naturally occurring mineral fiber that has been used in a wide variety of products as an insulator and fire-retardant. Possible sources of asbestos include the following: • Insulation in attics and attic-like spaces (e.g., vermiculite). • Wall insulation (e.g., vermiculite, insulation blocks). • Hot water and steam pipes coated with asbestos material or covered with an asbestos blanket or tape. • Oil and coal furnaces and door gaskets with asbestos insulation. • Vinyl flooring (including 9"-by-9" or 12"-by-12" floor tiles, vinyl sheet flooring, and the mastics and other adhesives used to secure the flooring). • Cement sheet, millboard and paper used as insulation around furnaces and wood- or coal-burning appliances. • Soundproofing or decorative surface materials sprayed on walls or ceilings, including popcorn ceilings. • Patching, joint compounds and textured paints on walls and ceilings. • Roofing, shingles and siding (including cement or adhesives). • Transite (cement and asbestos) combustion vent or transite flue. • Original plaster or plaster that is old enough to potentially contain asbestos. **Further Reading** Priority Issue 4.0 Asbestos	**Regular Inspections** As required under 40 CFR Part 763, Subpart E, asbestos-containing material (ACM) within the school should be periodically inspected (every 6 months) to ensure it is undisturbed and undamaged. **System and Building Operations** Ensure the school's AHERA asbestos management plan is maintained in accordance with federal law pursuant to 40 CFR Part 763, Subpart E. **Administrator and Staff Education** As required under 40 CFR Part 763, Subpart E, if the presence of asbestos has been documented in the school, ensure that school administrators, staff and the school nurse are educated on the dangers of asbestos and are aware of areas where ACM may be found so they can notify the facility manager of signs of damage or disturbance.

---

a. EPA, Asbestos, Learn About Asbestos

Priority IAQ Concern	Health Effects and Potential Exposure Locations	IAQ Considerations After the Building Upgrade
Lead	**Health Effects** Exposure to lead can cause learning difficulties, behavior problems, hearing damage, and in extreme cases, seizures or death. Children younger than 6 years of age and pregnant women are at greatest risk and should not be exposed to lead under any circumstances.[b] **Potential Exposure Locations** Lead was commonly used in paint before the 1978 Consumer Products Safety Commission ban on lead-based paint for applications for which consumers may be exposed. School-related sources of lead include flaking or peeling lead-based paint on the building interior and exterior, lead in dust, lead in soil, and lead in drinking water. ***Note*** *If there are concerns about lead in drinking water, see EPA's website* Drinking Water in Schools & Child Care Facilities **Further Reading** Priority Issue 5.0 Lead	**Regular Inspections** Regularly inspect known locations of lead, especially lead-based paint, for signs of wear, damage or flaking; promptly and safely address any deterioration. Prior to repair or maintenance activity that may disturb paint, the paint must be assessed to determine whether it is lead-based or assumed to be lead-based, and proper (required) precautions must be taken. See Priority Issue 5.0 Lead. **Administrator and Staff Education** If the presence of lead has been documented in the school, ensure that school administrators, staff and the school nurse are educated on the dangers of lead and areas where lead may be found so that they can notify facility managers of signs of damage or disturbance. **Student Education Opportunities for Teachers** Educate students about the health effects of lead. See EPA's Teacher Resources and Lesson Plans website for resources on lead. http://www.epa.gov/students/teachers.html

b. EPA, Indoor Air Quality, Lead Health Effects

Priority IAQ Concern	Health Effects and Potential Exposure Locations	IAQ Considerations After the Building Upgrade
Polychlorinated Biphenyls (PCBs)	**Health Effects** PCBs have been shown to cause a variety of adverse health effects, including effects on the immune system, reproductive system, nervous system and endocrine system in animals. PCBs also have been shown to cause cancer in animals. Studies in humans provide supportive evidence for the potential carcinogenic and non-carcinogenic effects of PCBs.[c] **Potential Exposure Locations** PCBs were manufactured domestically from 1929 until 1979, when EPA banned the processing or use of PCBs, except in totally enclosed equipment. [d] PCBs can be found in older buildings in fluorescent light ballast capacitors and potting material, electrical transformers, window caulking, rubberized paint formulations, and soil near the building. **Further Reading** Priority Issue 6.0 Polychlorinated Biphenyls (PCBs)	**Regular Inspections** If PCB-containing ballasts were not replaced as part of the building improvement project, inspect them regularly for any signs of wear or damage. **System and Building Operations** Intact, operational ballasts may not pose a health risk or environmental hazard; however, given that PCB-containing ballasts have not been manufactured domestically since 1979, the typical life expectancy of magnetic fluorescent light ballasts (10 to 15 years) has been well exceeded.[e] Also, PCB-containing ballasts may lack thermal overload protection, increasing the possibility of fires or leaks. The hazard can be worsened if the ballasts are mishandled by personnel who are unaware of the presence of PCBs in the lighting ballasts. **Administrator and Staff Education** Ensure that teachers and administrators understand where PCB-containing ballasts are located so they can warn the facility manager of damage. **Student Education Opportunities for Teachers** Educate students about PCBs. See EPA Fact Sheets for Schools and Teachers About PCB-Contaminated Caulk. Also see EPA's PCB-Containing Light Ballasts Web page.
Radon	**Health Effects** In the United States, radon is the leading cause of lung cancer among nonsmokers and the second-leading cause of lung cancer overall (after smoking), accounting for 21,000 deaths annually.[f] **Potential Exposure Locations** Radon is a naturally occurring, radioactive component in soil gas that enters buildings through floors and walls that are in contact with the ground. For schools, EPA recommends radon testing for all frequently occupied rooms in contact with the ground. **Further Reading** Priority Issue 7.0 Radon	**Regular Inspections** The only way to determine whether schools have elevated radon levels is to perform radon testing. If radon mitigation strategies were implemented for the school, periodically check to ensure that radon mitigation systems are operating properly and that ventilation systems are providing the required amount of outdoor ventilation air. Biennial retesting for radon should be performed in all areas of the schools that have been mitigated. **Student Education Opportunities for Teachers** Educate students about the health effects of radon. See EPA's Teacher Resources and Lesson Plans Web page for resources on radon. Also, see EPA's Radon Kids, Students and Teachers Web page for educational information and opportunities including the national radon poster contest for students.

c. EPA, PCBs, Health Effects of PCBs
d. EPA, PCBs, Basic Information
e. EPA, PCBs, PCB-Containing Fluorescent Light Ballasts (FLBs) in School Buildings
f. EPA, Radon, Health Risks

Priority IAQ Concern	Health Effects and Potential Exposure Locations	IAQ Considerations After the Building Upgrade
Belowground Vapor-Forming Contaminants (Except Radon)	**Health Effects** Common belowground contaminants include the following: **Volatile Organic Compounds** (VOCs) from gasoline components (benzene); dry cleaning and degreasing solvents, such as perchloroethylene and trichloroethylene; and building products, such as adhesives, sealants, paints and coatings. VOCs can cause eye, nose and throat irritation; headaches, fatigue, dizziness, loss of coordination and nausea; and damage to the liver, kidney and central nervous system. Some organics can cause cancer in animals; some are suspected or known to cause cancer in humans and have been associated with birth defects.[g] **Petroleum hydrocarbons** in soils can be caused by spills or leaks from oil and fuel storage tanks commonly associated with gas stations or fuel storage tank systems and piping. Petroleum hydrocarbons include many compounds, each having different health effects. Health effects can include headaches and dizziness from airborne exposure; numbness in the feet and legs; and various effects on the blood, immune system, lungs, skin and eyes.[h] **Metals:** Although low background levels of metals may not represent a health concern, elevated levels of some metals in soil are frequently encountered across the country, particularly in urban areas, and some (such as mercury) can form a hazardous vapor. **Potential Exposure Locations** Belowground contaminants can affect soil and groundwater, both of which can allow contaminants to enter buildings via direct seepage or vapor migration through building assemblies in contact with the ground, by tracking in on shoes, or direct skin/mouth/nose contact with such soils or related dusts. **Further Reading** Priority Issue 8.0 Belowground Vapor-Forming Contaminants	**Regular Inspections** If a venting system is installed to reduce vapor intrusion, performance monitoring of the system is equally important. If residual underground soil and ground water contamination exists, the school should retain an experienced environmental professional to develop a long-term monitoring plan and periodically complete testing around the school to document that the system is operating properly.

g. EPA, Indoor Air, Volatile Organic Compounds (VOCs)

h. ATSDR, Toxic Substances Portal—Total Petroleum Hydrocarbons (TPH)

Priority IAQ Concern	Health Effects and Potential Exposure Locations	IAQ Considerations After the Building Upgrade
Vehicle Exhaust	**Health Effects** With sufficient concentrations and duration, pollutants from vehicle exhaust may increase the chance of cancer or other serious health effects. Diesel exhaust specifically can aggravate respiratory and cardiovascular disease and existing asthma. It also can cause acute respiratory symptoms, chronic bronchitis and decreased lung function, all of which children are more susceptible to. **Potential Exposure Locations** Exhaust emissions come from vehicles such as school buses, cars, delivery trucks, and motorcycles, as well as from equipment used for construction and grounds maintenance. Vehicle exhaust emissions can affect indoor health when these outdoor contaminants migrate indoors, as may occur when vehicles idle during student drop-off and pick-up or when HVAC outdoor air intakes are located near vehicle idling zones, drawing exhaust emissions into the building.[i] **Further Reading** Priority Issue 9.0 Vehicle Exhaust	**System and Building Operations** Consider strategies to reduce exhaust emissions (e.g., purchase cleaning equipment that does not have gas-powered engines). Consider no- and low-cost adjustments to limit exhaust emissions exposure: • Institute anti-idling policies for school buses and parents. • Consider the way buses currently queue for pick-up and drop-off to determine whether engine runtime can be reduced while buses wait for students to board. • Do not open windows near loading and unloading zones and consider moving loading zones so they are at least 25 feet from windows, doors and outdoor air intakes. **Administrator and Staff Education** Promote alternative transportation options outlined in *IAQ Tools for Schools*. For example, "school-pooling" programs encourage carpools, bike partners or "walking school buses" that reduce the number of vehicles on school grounds. Public transit buses may also be an appropriate option for some students or staff. **Student and Parent Education** **Signage Opportunity:** Remind parents that vehicle emissions can affect their children's health. **Example Text:** *"Vehicle exhaust can trigger asthma attacks and other respiratory symptoms. Please, do not idle your vehicle while waiting."* **Sign Locations:** Within sight of drop-off and pick-up zones. **Signage Opportunity:** Remind students where it is safe to wait for buses and other rides home. **Example Text:** *"Waiting Zone. Please wait here for your ride so you don't breathe in harmful vehicle exhaust."* **Sign Locations:** Locate in a safe waiting zone, at least 25 feet from areas with operating vehicles.

i. EPA, IAQ Reference Guide, Appendix I—Emissions from Motor Vehicles and Equipment

Priority IAQ Concern	Health Effects and Potential Exposure Locations	IAQ Considerations After the Building Upgrade
Local and Regional Ambient Air Quality	**Health Effects** Ozone, particulate matter, carbon monoxide, nitrogen oxides, sulfur dioxide and lead are some of the pollutants that can be found in outdoor air, and EPA has set national ambient air quality standards for these six pollutants. Exposure to these pollutants is associated with numerous effects on human health, including increased respiratory symptoms, heart and lung diseases, and premature death. **Potential Exposure Locations** There are many potential sources of outdoor air pollution, ranging from large-scale industries to small businesses located within neighborhoods; from outdoor wood boilers to a variety of transportation-related sources, such as roads and transit hubs; agricultural activities and myriad other land uses also affect outdoor air quality. **Further Reading** Priority Issue 10.0 Local and Regional Ambient Air Quality	**Regular Inspections** Regional air quality can be monitored daily on weather websites and at www.airnow.gov. Local air quality may also be affected by surrounding businesses, such as industrial zones, which may not register on the regional air-quality tracking websites. **System and Building Operations** For new and existing HVAC systems, ensure that filters are replaced and maintained according to the manufacturer's printed instructions. Schools located in areas that consistently have degraded outdoor air quality may consider outdoor air treatment, which may include particle filtration or other devices to clean the outdoor air before it enters occupied spaces. The HVAC manufacturer's printed recommendations should be followed. **Administrator and Staff Education** Ensure that teachers, staff and school nurses are aware of air quality advisory days. During air quality advisories, children should not play outside and may experience respiratory symptoms. The AirNow School Flag Program also can be used to alert school staff to the local air quality forecast and help them to take actions to protect students' health, especially those with asthma. School staff also can become involved with local ozone "watchdog" groups and review school practices to help keep ozone levels in check. **Student Education Opportunities for Teachers** EPA's Teacher's Air Quality Resources Web page provides a variety of options for educational curriculum and student activities related to ambient air quality. The AirNow School Flag Program also provides a variety of resources.

Priority IAQ Concern	Health Effects and Potential Exposure Locations	IAQ Considerations After the Building Upgrade
Pests	**Health Effects** Risks arise from pests and exposure to pesticides in school settings. Diseases may be transmitted by biting insects. Asthma attacks may occur from allergens or triggers from cockroach and rodent infestations. Staff and students may be unnecessarily exposed to pests and pesticides. **Potential Exposure Locations** Rodents, cockroaches, termites, birds, bats and other pests can be found in school buildings. Pests prefer warm, dry spaces with easy access to food and water. **Further Reading** Priority Issue 11.0 Pests	**Regular Inspections** Many tactics that prevent pest problems and pest-conducive conditions also contribute to water and energy conservation, indoor air quality, cost reduction and asset preservation. For example, effective door sweeps can reduce pest complaints by 65%, reduce infiltration of dirt and prevent escape of heat and conditioned air. Repairing leaking pipes prevents pest access to moisture and also reduces water consumption and costs. In-house or contracted professional pest manager should conduct a comprehensive inspection of all buildings for defects, including cracks, crevices and other pest entryways; food, moisture and shelter resources available to pests; moisture, pest or other damage to structural elements; termite earthen tunnels, pest fecal matter or other signs of pest activity; and so forth. The report of all defects should identify corrective actions. The inspection should be mapped on the site and floor plan. Use a written Integrated Pest Management (IPM) inspection checklist or form for periodic inspections, listing each building feature (e.g., foundation, eaves) and room to be inspected, including specific locations within features or rooms (e.g., vents, storage closets) to be included in the inspection, and specific conditions to be noted (e.g., repair, cleaning needs). Maintain legible records of inspection results, pest management actions and evaluations of results; keep these records for at least 3 years. Establish a timeline for completing corrective actions and evaluating results. **System and Building Operations** Schools should implement IPM tactics that include prevention, inspection, communication, biopesticide use, and judicious and careful use of pesticides when necessary. When a pest professional is needed, your school or school district may choose to have its IPM program certified or recognized. When seeking IPM certification, look for a widely recognized program that provides assistance in developing, maintaining, sustaining and evaluating your IPM program. Educate facility managers about IPM through training, brochures and other appropriate guidance. **Occupant Education** Ensure that all school occupants are notified well in advance of pesticide applications on school grounds and in the local area. **Signage Opportunity:** Post signs prior to pesticide use to notify school occupants. *Note* *Many states have notification laws when pesticides are used.* **Example Text:** *"Pesticides will be used in this area on [date]. Do not walk in this area between [application date] and [safe contact date, per manufacturer printed directions]."* **Sign Locations:** Space signs at regular intervals around pesticide application area. Before applying pesticide, mark off entire application area with yellow caution tape. Unless absolutely necessary, pesticides should *not* be applied when students are present on campus. **Occupant Feedback** Provide a simple process for school administrators, staff and students to notify the facility manager if they see signs of pest infestations. Many schools use pest logs to record pest sightings; these logs often are located in the teachers' lounge. **Student Education Opportunities for Teachers** Educate students about IPM. See EPA's Teacher Resources and Lesson Plans Web page for links to resources on IPM.

Priority IAQ Concern	Health Effects and Potential Exposure Locations	IAQ Considerations After the Building Upgrade
Tracked-In Pollutants	**Health Effects** A variety of pollutants can be tracked into the school including dirt (which may be contaminated with other pollutants) and moisture. Potential health effects will depend on the composition of the tracked-in pollutants. **Potential Exposure Locations** Schools have especially high levels of occupant movement between inside and outside spaces, causing dirt, particulates and moisture to be tracked into the building. **Further Reading** Priority Issue 12.0 Tracked-In Pollutants	**System and Building Operations** During occupancy, tracked-in dirt and moisture can be reduced by using entryway systems as outlined in Priority Issue 12.0. Systems should be 10 feet long in the primary direction of travel to maximize the number of steps and potential for the system to remove dirt and moisture. There are two common types of entryway systems: • **Roll-out mats** require less upfront cost but must be vacuumed daily and fully cleaned regularly, at least once a week. • **Built-in systems** include a scraper surface to clean shoes, followed by an absorption surface and a finishing surface. **Occupant Education** **Signage Opportunity:** Remind occupants and visitors to clean shoes carefully. **Example Text:** *"Help keep our school clean! Wiping your feet helps to keep allergens and asthma triggers outside and reduces maintenance and cleaning costs!"* **Sign Locations:** Place at all building entrances.
Building Products/Materials Emissions	**Health Effects** VOCs can cause eye, nose, and throat irritation; headaches, fatigue, dizziness, loss of coordination and nausea; and damage to the liver, kidney, and central nervous system. Some organics can cause cancer in animals; some are suspected or known to cause cancer in humans and have been associated with birth defects.[j] **Potential Exposure Locations** VOCs are found in many products and materials used in and around schools, including paints; carpets and pads; composite wood products; cleaning supplies; art, science and vocational education materials and processes; air fresheners; and furniture. **Further Reading** Priority Issue 13.0 Building Products/Materials Emissions	**System and Building Operations** When performing minor touch-up or repair projects, meet the VOC guidance outlined in Priority Issue 13.0 Building Products/Materials Emissions and make sure to properly ventilate the space before and after work. Ensure that chemical storage rooms have exhaust ventilation. **Administrator and Staff Education** Ensure that teachers, administrators and maintenance staff know how to properly store hazardous chemicals, such as cleaning chemicals, pesticides and chemistry equipment. See EPA's Toolkit for Safe Chemical Management in K–12 Schools Web page, which gives K–12 schools information and tools to manage chemicals responsibly.

j. EPA, Indoor Air, Volatile Organic Compounds (VOCs)

Priority IAQ Concern	Health Effects and Potential Exposure Locations	IAQ Considerations After the Building Upgrade
Combustion Appliances (Vented and Unvented)	**Health Effects** Combustion pollutants result from the burning of fuels and other materials. Common combustion pollutants include carbon monoxide (CO), nitrogen dioxide (NO_2) and respirable particulate matter (PM). CO is a colorless, odorless gas. Symptoms of CO exposure may mimic influenza and include fatigue, headache, dizziness, nausea and vomiting, cognitive impairment, and tachycardia. At high concentrations CO exposure can be fatal. NO_2 is a colorless, odorless gas that causes eye, nose and throat irritation; shortness of breath; and an increased risk of respiratory infection. Health effects of respirable PM include eye, nose, and throat irritation; respiratory infections and bronchitis; asthma; and lung cancer. **Potential Exposure Locations** CO results from incomplete oxidation of carbon in combustion processes. Potential CO sources include improperly vented furnaces or combustion appliances, malfunctioning gas ranges, and exhaust fumes that have been drawn back into the building. Worn, improperly adjusted or poorly maintained combustion devices (e.g., boilers, furnaces), or a flue that is improperly sized, blocked, disconnected or leaking, can be significant sources. Auto, truck or bus exhaust from attached garages, nearby roads or idling vehicles in parking areas can also be sources. Sources of NO_2 and respirable PM include unvented or improperly vented combustion equipment, fireplaces, wood stoves and kerosene heaters, and diesel exhaust. **Further Reading** Priority Issue 14.0 Vented Combustion Appliances and Priority Issue 15.0 Unvented Combustion Appliances	**Regular Inspections** Maintenance staff should perform regular inspections of combustion appliances and associated venting systems, as well as of carbon monoxide detection and warning equipment, to ensure that equipment is in good condition and operating properly. **System and Building Operations** Combustion equipment must be maintained to ensure that there are no blockages, and air and fuel mixtures must be properly adjusted to ensure complete combustion. If the school has carbon monoxide detection and warning equipment, follow manufacturer calibration recommendations to make sure that they are working properly. Additional ventilation can be used as a temporary measure when elevated levels of CO are experienced for short periods of time. **Occupant Education** **Signage Opportunity:** Educate occupants on the importance of CO detection and warning equipment. **Example Language:** *"Carbon monoxide (CO) is a colorless, odorless gas that can cause headaches, dizziness, disorientation, nausea and fatigue at low levels of exposure. At higher concentrations, CO exposure can be fatal. If this CO alarm provides a warning for a high CO level, vacate the room and notify the facility manager and school nurse immediately."* **Sign Locations:** Adjacent to each CO alarm.

Priority IAQ Concern	Health Effects and Potential Exposure Locations	IAQ Considerations After the Building Upgrade
Ozone From Indoor Sources	**Health Effects** Breathing ozone can trigger a variety of health problems, including decreases in lung function, aggravation of asthma, throat irritation and cough, chest pain and shortness of breath, inflammation of lung tissue, and increased susceptibility to respiratory infection.[k] **Potential Exposure Locations** Ozone can be generated by equipment within the school, such as photocopiers and laser printers, and portable air cleaning devices designed to intentionally produce ozone. **Further Reading** Priority Issue 16.0 Ozone From Indoor Sources	**System and Building Operations** Ensure that air-cleaning devices designed to intentionally produce ozone are not introduced into the building, including portable air cleaners. Periodically assess ventilation and exhaust in areas with office equipment that generates ozone (e.g., copiers and printers). Follow manufacturers' printed instructions for maintenance of office equipment that has ozone capture equipment (e.g., active carbon filter). **Administrator and Staff Education** Ensure that staff do not bring portable air cleaning devices that are designed to intentionally produce ozone into the school. **Student Education Opportunities for Teachers** Educate students about the health effects of ozone. See EPA's Teacher Resources and Lesson Plans Web page for a link to the educational material, "Ozone: Good Up High, Bad Nearby."
Environmental Tobacco Smoke	**Health Effects** Environmental tobacco smoke, sometimes referred to as "secondhand smoke," has been classified as a Group A carcinogen by EPA. It also has been associated with multiple health effects in children, including the onset of asthma, increased severity of or difficulty in controlling asthma, frequent upper respiratory infections, middle-ear infections, and pneumonia and bronchitis. **Potential Exposure Locations** Tobacco smoke will be found in schools only if smoking occurs on school property. **Further Reading** Priority Issue 17.0 Environmental Tobacco Smoke	**Administrator and Staff Education** Federal regulations (20 USC Section 6083) prohibit smoking within any indoor facility owned or leased or contracted for and used for provision of routine or regular kindergarten, elementary or secondary education or library services to children. State or local laws may be more restrictive. Urge teachers, administrators and staff to make the school's tobacco-use policy a priority. The policy must be consistent with local and state laws and should include prohibitions against tobacco use by students, all school staff, parents and visitors on school property; in school vehicles; and at school-sponsored functions away from school property. **Occupant Education** **Signage Opportunity:** Remind occupants and visitors of the school's smoking policy. **Example Text:** *"To protect the health of students and staff, this is a smoke-free school. Smoking is not permitted anywhere on school grounds."* **Sign Locations:** Space evenly around the building perimeter, and especially next to doors, windows and outdoor air intakes.

k. EPA, Indoor Air, Ozone Generators that are Sold as Air Cleaners

Priority IAQ Concern	Health Effects and Potential Exposure Locations	IAQ Considerations After the Building Upgrade
Heating, Ventilation, & Air-Conditioning (HVAC) Outdoor Air Ventilation	**Health Effects** Poorly designed or maintained HVAC systems can exacerbate IAQ problems. For example, moisture can accumulate in ducts leading to mold growth, incorrectly installed or maintained filters can allow particulates to be spread throughout the building, and systems that do not provide enough outdoor air ventilation can result in high levels of indoor pollutants, often as indicated by elevated indoor carbon dioxide levels, which is considered a surrogate for other indoor pollutants. This will contribute to occupant dissatisfaction and can cause headaches, dizziness, nausea, poor concentration, lethargy and reduced student performance. Inadequate indoor thermal control also can negatively affect student performance. **HVAC Opportunities** Among the main purposes of an HVAC system are to help maintain good IAQ through adequate ventilation and filtration and to provide thermal comfort and indoor moisture control. HVAC systems are among the largest energy consumers in schools. The choice and design of the HVAC system can also affect many other high-performance goals, including water consumption (water-cooled air conditioning equipment) and acoustics. Engineers can design a quality system that is cost-competitive with traditional ventilation designs while successfully providing an appropriate quantity and quality of outdoor air, lowering energy costs, allowing for easier maintenance, and improving student performance. **Further Reading** Priority Issue 18.0 HVAC Equipment and Priority Issue 19.0 Outdoor Air Ventilation	**Regular Inspections** Create a maintenance schedule for the HVAC system to ensure that filters are changed regularly and any calibration requirements are met. **System and Building Operations** If HVAC systems are upgraded or improved during the construction project, the contracting team must provide thorough, onsite training to the facility management staff to ensure systems can be operated properly. Facility managers are encouraged to pay special attention to the sequence of operations, any direct digital controls or building automation systems, and the outdoor air ventilation rates that the system is designed to provide to each room. When natural ventilation is provided, efforts should be made to ensure that windows and other ventilation openings are operated appropriately to ensure adequate ventilation. **Occupant Feedback** Provide a system for school occupants to comment on perceived indoor air quality, thermal comfort, humidity levels, standing water or leaks, and air speed, as these issues can be indicators of HVAC calibration or operational problems.

Priority IAQ Concern	Health Effects and Potential Exposure Locations	IAQ Considerations After the Building Upgrade
Exhaust Ventilation	**Health Effects** Although schools can use HVAC systems to control moisture and dilute pollutants, rooms with significant moisture generation or rooms with strong, localized sources of pollutants (e.g., where VOC-containing products are stored or used) often require exhaust systems to ensure adequate IAQ. The health effects that often can be reduced by dedicated exhaust systems are documented in the preceding sections of this appendix: "Moisture Control and Mold," "Building Products/ Materials Emissions," and "Vented Combustion Appliances and Unvented Combustion Appliances." **Potential Exposure Locations** Locker rooms, bathrooms, laundries and other areas with frequent levels of high humidity are at increased risk of mold and mildew. Examples of spaces with strong, localized contaminant sources include art rooms, science laboratories, kitchens, woodwork shops, machine shops and janitors' closets. Building improvement projects may use adhesives, sealants, paints and coatings that contain VOCs in high concentrations. **Further Reading** Priority Issue 20.0 Exhaust Ventilation	**Administrator and Staff Education** Ensure that teachers, administrators and maintenance staff know where to store chemicals, especially if storage closets with dedicated exhaust systems are located in the school. Teachers and staff who regularly store and use chemicals should have information on EPA Toolkit for Safe Chemical Management in K–12 Schools **Occupant Feedback** Provide a system for school occupants to communicate moisture and odor complaints, as complaints may stem from deficient exhaust systems.

Priority IAQ Concern	Health Effects and Potential Exposure Locations	IAQ Considerations After the Building Upgrade
Mercury	**Health Effects** Mercury is a neurotoxic substance that can produce a wide range of health effects in children depending on the amount and timing of exposure. Elemental (metallic) mercury primarily causes health effects when it is inhaled as a vapor and absorbed into the lungs. **Potential Exposure Locations** Mercury is used in many items found in schools, such as thermometers, barometers, switches, thermostats, flow meters, fluorescent lighting and compact fluorescent light bulbs, and laboratory reagents in chemistry and science laboratories. Two major causes of mercury releases and spills at schools are improper storage and mishandling of these items, which can result in the release of mercury via breakage or spillage. **Further Reading** Priority Issue 21.0 Building Safety for Children and Other Occupants	**System and Building Operations** Ensure that the school has a mercury spill response plan. Properly dispose of fluorescent lighting and compact fluorescent light bulbs. **Administrator and Staff Education** Ensure that teachers, administrators and maintenance staff know how to properly store and handle mercury compounds and mercury-containing equipment and components. **Student Education Opportunities for Teachers** Educate students about the potential health hazards of mercury. See EPA's Mercury: An Educator's Toolkit Web page.

Appendix C: Worker Protection

Priority Issue 23.0 Jobsite Safety of the Energy Savings Plus Health Guide refers to this appendix for worker protection. This appendix contains information to help those performing and supervising the building upgrade assess the risks to workers; it recommends actions to minimize risks to workers' health and safety and identifies resources for additional information.

Worker protection is especially important in older buildings. Areas undergoing construction may contain remnants of legacy contaminants, such as lead and asbestos. Although these materials often are not considered harmful if left undisturbed or covered, they can become a concern when disturbed. Therefore, it is essential that the contractors review available informa-tion about the existence of such materials before beginning any modifications to the building. If existence of hazardous materials is suspected, a review must be commissioned by the school authorities. In some situations, only certified personnel can perform certain activities outlined in this Guide.

By law, employers and supervisors are required to provide workers with a workplace that is free from recognized hazards that are causing or are likely to cause death or serious physical harm, as required in Section 5(a)(1) of the Occupational Safety and Health Act of 1970. Employers and supervisors must ensure the following:

1. Work site operations are conducted in compliance with Occupational Safety and Health Administration (OSHA) regulatory requirements. OSHA regulatory requirements identify the following construction hazards to be addressed:

Asbestos-Containing Materials	29 CFR Part 1926.1101 and 40 CFR Part 763, Subpart G
Chemical Hazards	29 CFR Part 1910.1200
Confined Spaces	29 CFR Part 1926.21 (b)(6)(i)
Electrical	29 CFR Part 1926, Subpart K
Falls	29 CFR Part 1926.501
Ladders	29 CFR Part 1926.1053
Lead	29 CFR Part 1926.62 and 40 CFR 745
Personal Protective Equipment	29 CFR Part 1926.28

2. Workers are trained in the hazards of their job and the methods to protect themselves.

3. Workers are provided the protective equipment needed to reduce site exposures. Employers are required to perform a Personal Protective Equipment Hazard Assessment for each employee.

Table C1 provides a list of recommended assessments and actions for worker safety concerns. Project contract documents (drawings or specifications) and site plans should include precautions to address these issues. Table C1 also includes measures an employer needs to take to evaluate existing and potential health concerns and recommended actions to ensure worker safety. Assistance with developing these worker protection plans often is available from state or federal training programs. OSHA offers training courses and educational programs to help broaden worker and employer knowledge on the recognition, avoidance, and prevention of safety and health hazards in their workplaces. OSHA also offers training and educational materials that help businesses train their workers and comply with the Occupational Safety and Health Act (see http://www.osha.gov/dte/index.html).

When known pollutants are being produced or disturbed during retrofit activities, follow appropriate standards (including OSHA, National Institute for Occupational Safety and Health [NIOSH] and EPA standards) to minimize worker and occupant exposure. The document "IAQ Guidelines for Occupied Buildings Under Construction" published by the Sheet Metal and Air Conditioning Contractors' National Association (SMACNA) also can be used as a best-practices manual for maintaining IAQ in occupied buildings undergoing renovation or construction. The SMACNA document covers how to manage the source of air pollutants, control measures, quality control and documentation, and communication with occupants.

Table C1: Recommended Assessments and Actions for Worker Safety Concerns

Asbestos

Assessment: Determine whether workers will be exposed to ACM. Because of the predominant use of ACM, construction and renovation activities in older schools may expose workers to this hazard. The Asbestos Hazard Emergency Response Act (AHERA), a provision of the Toxic Substances Control Act, became law in 1986. AHERA requires local education agencies to inspect their schools for ACMs and prepare management plans to prevent or reduce asbestos hazards, often known as an AHERA asbestos management plan.

Actions

- Comply with the ACM in Schools Rule at 40 CFR Part 763, Subpart E and the OSHA rule at 29 CFR Part 1926.1101, which provides the required protection measures for work involving ACMs.
- See OSHA's website on asbestos for additional information and resources.

Chemical Hazards

Assessment: Determine whether workers will be exposed to chemical hazards[I] by chemicals in use, accidentally released by actions taken (e.g., spills from mercury-containing lamps or ballasts), or contact with pre-existing chemically contaminated building materials, subsoils or vapors.

Actions

- Comply with the OSHA rule at 29 CFR Part 1910.1200, which includes the following requirements (not an exhaustive list):

  o that chemical content information be made available for all chemicals in use;

  o that containers be properly labeled; and

  o that workers handling chemicals be properly informed and trained.

- Use chemicals that are best-in-class for the particular application in terms of having low toxic content and/or low contaminant emissions. Examples include paints, adhesives, sealants and coatings that meet the emissions criteria of California Department of Public Health Specification 01350.
- Proper health and safety precautions should be employed by workers who use or may come in contact with pesticides or chemical contaminants in building materials, subsoils or vapors.
- For pesticides, comply with EPA's 40 Code of Federal Regulations Part 170—Current Agricultural Worker Protection Standard (includes all amendments as of October 3, 1997).
- See OSHA's website on chemical hazards communication for additional information and resources.

Confined Spaces

Assessment: Determine whether workers will be exposed to confined-space hazards.

Actions

- Ensure the work space is cleaned regularly and has adequate ventilation and exhaust and that construction is phased properly to protect workers and occupants from construction activities that are considered high risk, as outlined in SMACNA "IAQ Guidelines for Occupied Buildings Under Construction," 2nd Edition.
- Under OSHA rule at 29 CFR Part 1926.21 (b)(6)(i), inform all employees required to enter confined or enclosed spaces about the following:

  o the nature of the hazards involved;

  o the necessary precautions to be taken; and

  o the use of required protective and emergency equipment.

- See OSHA's website on confined spaces for additional resources on confined space hazards in general industry.
- See OSHA's "Protect Yourself: Carbon Monoxide Poisoning" Quick Card for additional information on sources of CO and recommended actions for preventing CO exposure.
- See Priority Issue 13.0 Building Products/Materials Emissions and EPA's Design for the Environment Program website for more information on selecting less toxic products and materials that may be used in confined spaces.

Dust

Assessment: Determine whether the work will generate dust. Use best-practice measures to manage and control air quality contaminants in areas of work.

Actions

- Educate workers about dust containment procedures and how to control dust and debris created by equipment used in construction activities.
- Use work methods that minimize dust and prevent dust from spreading to other areas of the school.
- Isolate areas where work is being performed (e.g., sealed with plastic sheeting) to contain any dust that is generated during construction activities.
- Remove all classroom furniture from the work area or cover furniture with plastic sheeting to prevent dust contamination.
- Turn off forced-air, central heating and air-conditioning systems (including local, window air conditioning units) while work that creates dust is being completed.
- Collect and remove all construction debris.
- Conduct a careful cleanup routinely and at the end of the project.
- See OSHA's websites on wood dust, combustible dust, and permissible exposure limits for additional information and resources.

I. Based on 29 CFR Part 1926.59, a chemical hazard is a chemical that is either a physical hazard or a health hazard. "Physical hazard" refers to a chemical for which there is scientifically valid evidence that it is a combustible liquid, a compressed gas, explosive, flammable, an organic peroxide, an oxidizer, pyrophoric, unstable (reactive) or water-reactive. "Health hazard" refers to a chemical for which there is statistically significant evidence based on at least one study conducted in accordance with established scientific principles that acute or chronic health effects may occur in exposed employees.

Table C1: Recommended Assessments and Actions for Worker Safety Concerns (continued)

Electrical

Assessment: Determine whether workers will be exposed to electrical hazards.

Actions

- Follow OSHA rule 29 CFR Part 1926, Subpart K requirements for protecting workers from electrical hazards (not an exhaustive list):
  - o Employers must make sure that all non-double-insulated electric equipment is equipped with a grounding conductor (three-wire type).
  - o Worn or frayed electric cords must not be used.
  - o Employers must provide either ground-fault circuit interrupters or an assured equipment grounding conductor program (which includes the regular testing of all equipment grounding conductors) to protect employees from ground faults.

- See OSHA's Electrical Incidents E-Tool for additional information on electrical safety.

Falls

Assessment: Determine whether workers will be required to work at heights of 6 feet or more.

Actions

- If work is required at heights of 6 feet or more, protect workers with guard rails or by properly securing to prevent falls.

- See OSHA rule at 29 CFR Part 1926.501 for additional information on requirements.

- See OSHA's Web page on fall protection and OSHA's Falls E-Tool for additional information on protecting workers from fall hazards.

Ladders

Assessment: Determine whether workers will be using ladders.

Actions:

- Follow OSHA rule at 29 CFR Part 1926.1053, which includes the following requirements (not an exhaustive list):
  - o Portable ladders must be able to support at least four times the maximum intended load.
  - o Ladders that must lean against a wall are to be positioned at a 4:1 angle.
  - o Ladders are to be kept free of oil, grease, wet paint and other slipping hazards.
  - o The area around the top and bottom of the ladder must be kept clear.
  - o Ladders must not be tied or fastened together to provide longer sections.
  - o Metal ladders must not be used while working on electrical equipment and electrical wiring.

- See the OSHA rule at 29 CFR Part 1926.1053 for additional information on requirements.
- See OSHA's publication, "Stairways and Ladders: A Guide to OSHA Rules," for additional resources on ladder safety.

Lead

Assessment: Determine whether project activities will expose workers to lead dust according to the Assessment Protocols outlined in the Priority Issue 5.0 Lead. The most common lead hazards in schools are lead-based paint (especially in pre-1978 buildings), lead dust and contaminated soil. Other sources of lead hazards are older plumbing fixtures, vinyl miniblinds, painted toys and furniture made before 1978, lead smelters, or other industrial sources.

Actions

- If the facility was built before 1978, the existing paint is assumed to contain lead, and retrofitting or renovation activities must comply with EPA's Renovation, Repair and Painting Program Rule (40 CFR Part 745) and the OSHA rule at 29 CFR Part 1926.62. See EPA's EPA Renovation, Repair and Painting Program Rule website for additional information.

- See OSHA's publication, "Lead in Construction," for information on OSHA requirements to protect workers from lead hazards in the construction industry.

Mold

Assessment: Determine whether workers will be exposed to mold.

Actions

- All suspected moldy areas should be remediated by properly trained individuals. Moisture problems need to be identified and fixed or mold will return. If mold is expected to be disturbed during activities, immediately bring this to the attention of the site manager and refer to OSHA's "A Brief Guide to Mold in the Workplace," NIOSH's "Recommendations for Cleaning and Remediation of Flood-Contaminated HVAC Systems: A Guide for Building Owners and Managers," EPA's "Mold Remediation in Schools and Commercial Buildings," the American Conference of Government Industrial Hygienists' "Bioaerosols Assessment and Control," the American Industrial Hygiene Association's "Recognition, Evaluation, and Control of Indoor Mold," or the Institute of Inspection, Cleaning and Restoration Certification's S520 "Standard and Reference Guide for Professional Mold Remediation."

- See EPA's Molds and Moisture website for additional information on mold and mold remediation.

Table C1: Recommended Assessments and Actions for Worker Safety Concerns (continued)

Polychlorinated Biphenyls (PCBs)	Spray Polyurethane Foam (SPF)
Assessment: Determine whether workers may be handling PCB-containing or PCB-contaminated building materials, including fluorescent light ballasts and caulk.	**Assessment:** Determine whether workers will be using SPF, which may contain chemicals such as isocyanates (e.g., methylene diphenyl diisocyanate), amines, flame retardants and/or other additives. There are three main types of SPF products (two-component high pressure, two-component low pressure, and one-component foam), each of which has different applications. Determine which of the three main types of SPF products will be used.

PCBs — Actions

- See EPA's PCB-Containing Fluorescent Light Ballasts in School Buildings Web page for information on proper maintenance, removal and disposal of PCB-containing fluorescent light ballasts. If leaking ballasts are discovered, wear protective clothing including chemical-resistant (nitrile) gloves, boots and disposable overalls.

- See EPA's PCBs in Caulk—Steps to Safe Renovation and Abatement of Buildings That Have PCB-Containing Caulk website for information on this topic. Work practices to help ensure worker and occupant safety include employing protective measures (both interior and exterior), complying with occupational protective regulations, communicating with building occupants/third parties, setting up the work area to prevent the spread of dust, using appropriate tools that minimize the generation of dust/heat, and leaving the work area clean.

SPF — Actions

- Applicators, crew and building occupants in the work area are required to use protective equipment to prevent exposure to isocyanates and other SPF chemicals. Protective equipment requirements vary depending on the type of SPF product.

- Review label and product information for ingredients, hazards, directions, safe work practices and precautions.

- Ensure health and safety training is completed and safe work practices are followed to prevent eye, skin and inhalation exposures during and after SPF installation.

- Exercise caution when determining a safe re-entry time for unprotected occupants and workers based on the manufacturer's printed recommendation. If you experience breathing problems or other adverse health effects from weatherizing with SPF, seek immediate medical attention.

- See OSHA's Green Job Hazards website for additional information on the hazards associated with SPF.

- See EPA's SPF website for additional information.

- See the American Chemistry Council's SPF Health and Safety website for additional information.

Abbreviations and Acronyms Used in Appendices

ACM – asbestos-containing material

AHERA – Asbestos Hazard Emergency Response Act

ANSI – American National Standards Institute

AP – assessment protocols

ASHRAE – American Society of Heating, Refrigerating and Air-Conditioning Engineers

CFR – Code of Federal Regulations

CO – carbon monoxide

EPA – U.S. Environmental Protection Agency

HVAC – Heating, Ventilation and Air Conditioning

IAQ – indoor air quality

IPM – integrated pest management

K–12 – kindergarten through 12th grade

MA – minimum actions

NIOSH – National Institute for Occupational Safety and Health

OPR – owner's project requirements

OSHA – Occupational Safety and Health Administration

PCBs – polychlorinated biphenyls

PM – particulate matter

SMACNA – Sheet Metal and Air Conditioning Contractors' National Association

SPF – spray polyurethane foam

VOC – volatile organic compound

Agency for Toxic Substances and Disease Registry: Toxic Substances Portal—Total Petroleum Hydrocarbons (TPH). 2014. http://www.atsdr.cdc.gov/toxfaqs/TF.asp?id=423&tid=75

American Chemistry Council: Spray Polyurethane Foam Health and Safety. http://www.spraypolyurethane.org

American Conference of Government Industrial Hygienists: Bioaerosols Assessment and Control. 1999. http://www.acgih.org/store/ProductDetail.cfm?id=349

American Industrial Hygiene Association: Recognition, Evaluation, and Control of Indoor Mold. 2008. https://webportal.aiha.org/Purchase/ProductDetail.aspx?Product_code=3f9e0a5a-4778-de11-96b0-0050568361fd

ASHRAE Standard 62.1: ANSI/ASHRAE Standard 62.1-2013. Ventilation for Acceptable Indoor Air Quality. 2013. http://www.techstreet.com/ashrae/products/1865968

ASHRAE Standard 189.1: ANSI/ASHRAE Standard 189.1-2011: Standard for the Design of High-Performance Green Buildings: Except Low-Rise Residential Buildings. 2011. American Society of Heating, Refrigeration and Air-Conditioning Engineers. https://www.ashrae.org/resources--publications/bookstore/standard-189-1

California Department of Public Health, Emission Testing Method for California Specification 01350: Standard Method for the Testing and Evaluation of Volatile Organic Chemical Emissions From Indoor Sources Using Environmental Chambers, Version 1.1. 2010. http://www.cdph.ca.gov/programs/IAQ/Documents/cdph-iaq_standardmethod_v1_1_2010%20new1110.pdf

CDC (Centers for Disease Control and Prevention), NIOSH (National Institute for Occupational Safety and Health): CDC NIOSH website. http://www.cdc.gov/niosh

CDC, NIOSH: Storm, Flood, and Hurricane Response: Recommendations for the Cleaning and Remediation of Flood-Contaminated HVAC Systems: A Guide for Building Owners and Managers. 2010. http://www.cdc.gov/niosh/topics/emres/cleaning-flood-HVAC.html

EPA (U.S. Environmental Protection Agency): AirNow School Flag Program: Know Your Air Quality To Protect Students Health. http://www.airnow.gov/index.cfm?action=school_flag_program.index

EPA: AirNow. http://www.airnow.gov/

EPA: AirNow Teacher's Air Quality Resources. 2014. http://www.airnow.gov/index.cfm?action=learning.forteachers

EPA: An Introduction to Indoor Air Quality (IAQ). Lead (Pb). Lead Health Effects. 2012. http://www.epa.gov/iaq/lead.html#Health_Effects

EPA: An Introduction to Indoor Air Quality (IAQ): Volatile Organic Compounds (VOCs). 2012. http://www.epa.gov/iaq/voc.html

EPA: Asbestos. Learn About Asbestos. Health Effects From Exposure to Asbestos. 2014. http://www2.epa.gov/asbestos/learn-about-asbestos#effects

EPA: Design for the Environment. 2014. http://www.epa.gov/dfe

EPA: Design for the Environment. Labeled Products and Our Partners. 2014. http://epa.gov/dfe/pubs/projects/formulat/formpart.htm

EPA: Drinking Water in Schools & Child Care Facilities. 2012. http://water.epa.gov/infrastructure/drinkingwater/schools/index.cfm

EPA: *IAQ Tools for Schools*. IAQ Reference Guide, Appendix H: Mold and Moisture. 2012. http://www.epa.gov/iaq/schools/tfs/guideh.html

EPA: *IAQ Tools for Schools*. IAQ Reference Guide, Appendix I: Emissions from Motor Vehicles and Equipment. 2012. http://www.epa.gov/iaq/schools/tfs/guidei.html

EPA: Indoor Air. Ozone Generators That Are Sold as Air Cleaners. 2013. http://www.epa.gov/iaq/pubs/ozonegen.html#table%201

EPA: Lead. Renovation, Repair and Painting Program. http://www2.epa.gov/lead/renovation-repair-and-painting-program

EPA: Mercury: An Educator's Toolkit. 2012. http://www.epa.gov/region7/mercury/educator_toolkit.htm

EPA: Mold and Moisture. Introduction to Mold and Mold Remediation for Environmental and Public Health Professionals Course. 2012. http://www.epa.gov/mold/moldcourse/

EPA: Mold and Moisture. Mold Remediation in Schools and Commercial Buildings. 2008. http://www.epa.gov/mold/mold_remediation.html

EPA: Molds and Moisture. 2013.
http://www.epa.gov/mold/

EPA: Pesticides Health and Safety: Current Agricultural Worker Protection Standard. 2014. http://www.epa.gov/pesticides/safety/workers/PART170.htm

EPA: Polychlorinated Biphenyls (PCBs). Basic Information: Polychlorinated Biphenyls (PCBs). 2013. http://www.epa.gov/epawaste/hazard/tsd/pcbs/pubs/about.htm

EPA: Polychlorinated Biphenyls (PCBs). Fact Sheets for Schools and Teachers About PCB-Contaminated Caulk. 2012. http://www.epa.gov/pcbsincaulk/caulkschoolkit.htm

EPA: Polychlorinated Biphenyls (PCBs). Health Effects of PCBs. 2013. http://www.epa.gov/epawaste/hazard/tsd/pcbs/pubs/effects.htm

EPA: Polychlorinated Biphenyls (PCBs). PCB-Containing Fluorescent Light Ballasts (FLBs) in School Buildings: A Guide for School Administrators and Maintenance Personnel. 2013. http://www.epa.gov/epawaste/hazard/tsd/pcbs/pubs/ballasts.htm

EPA: Polychlorinated Biphenyls (PCBs): Steps to Safe Renovation and Abatement of Buildings That Have PCB-Containing Caulk. 2012.
http://www.epa.gov/pcbsincaulk/guide/index.htm

EPA: Radon. Health Risks. 2012.
http://www.epa.gov/radon/healthrisks.html

EPA: Radon. Kids, Students and Teachers. 2013.
http://www.epa.gov/radon/justforkids.html

EPA: Toolkit for Safe Chemical Management in Schools. 2012. http://www.epa.gov/schools/guidelinestools/toolkit.html

EPA: Spray Polyurethane Foam (SPF) Home. 2013.
http://www.epa.gov/dfe/pubs/projects/spf/spray_polyurethane_foam.html

EPA: State School Environmental Health Guidelines. 2012.
http://www.epa.gov/schools/guidelinestools/ehguide/

EPA: Teacher Resources and Lesson Plans. 2012.
http://www.epa.gov/students/teachers.html

EPA: Teacher Resources and Lesson Plans. Hold the Mold.
http://www.epa.gov/students/pdf/holdthemold.pdf

Institute of Inspection, Cleaning and Restoration Certification: BSR-IICRC S520 Mold Remediation. Standard and Reference Guide for Professional Mold Remediation. 2008.
http://www.iicrc.org/standards/iicrc-s520/

OSHA (Occupational Safety and Health Administration): U.S. Department of Labor OSHA website. http://www.osha.gov

OSHA, 29 CFR Part 1910.1200: Subpart Z. Hazard Communication. Occupational Safety and Health Standards: Toxic and Hazardous Substances. https://www.osha.gov/pls/oshaweb/owadisp.show_document?p_table=standards&p_id=10099

OSHA, 29 CFR Part 1926.21: Safety Training and Education. Safety and Health Regulations for Construction: General Safety and Health Provisions. https://www.osha.gov/pls/oshaweb/owadisp.show_document?p_table=STANDARDS&p_id=10607

OSHA, 29 CFR Part 1926.28: Subpart C. Personal Protective Equipment. Safety and Health Regulations for Construction: General Safety and Health Provisions. http://www.osha.gov/pls/oshaweb/owadisp.show_document?p_table=STANDARDS&p_id=10614

OSHA, 29 CFR Part 1926.62: Subpart D. Lead. Safety and Health Regulations for Construction: Occupational Health and Environmental Controls http://www.osha.gov/pls/oshaweb/owadisp.show_document?p_table=STANDARDS&p_id=10641

OSHA, 29 CFR Part 1926: Subpart K. Electrical. Safety and Health Regulations for Construction. http://www.osha.gov/pls/oshaweb/owadisp.show_document?p_table=STANDARDS&p_id=10915

OSHA, 29 CFR Part 1926.501: Subpart M. Duty to Have Fall Protection. Safety and Health Regulations for Construction. http://www.osha.gov/pls/oshaweb/owadisp.show_document?p_id=10757&p_table=STANDARDS

OSHA, 29 CFR Part 1926.1053: Subpart X. Ladders. Safety and Health Regulations for Construction. http://www.osha.gov/pls/oshaweb/owadisp.show_document?p_table=standards&p_id=10839

OSHA, 29 CFR Part 1926.1101: Subpart Z. Asbestos. Safety and Health Regulations for Construction: Toxic and Hazardous Substances. http://www.osha.gov/pls/oshaweb/owadisp.show_document?p_id=10862&p_table=STANDARDS

OSHA: A Brief Guide to Mold in the Workplace.
http://www.osha.gov/dts/shib/shib101003.html

OSHA: Asbestos. http://www.osha.gov/SLTC/asbestos/

OSHA: Combustible Dust. An Explosion Hazard.
http://www.osha.gov/dsg/combustibledust/index.html

OSHA: Confined Spaces http://www.osha.gov/SLTC/confinedspaces/index.html

OSHA: Electrical Incidents E-Tool. http://www.osha.gov/SLTC/etools/construction/electrical_incidents/mainpage.html

OSHA: Fall Protection. http://www.osha.gov/SLTC/fallprotection/index.html

OSHA: Falls E-Tool. http://www.osha.gov/SLTC/etools/construction/falls/mainpage.html

OSHA: Green Jobs Hazards, Weather Insulating/Sealing.
http://www.osha.gov/dep/greenjobs/weather_spf.html

OSHA: Hazard Communication.
http://www.osha.gov/dsg/hazcom/index.html

OSHA: Lead. Construction.
http://www.osha.gov/SLTC/lead/construction.html

OSHA: Occupational Safety and Health Act of 1970. Section 5(a)(1). http://www.osha.gov/pls/oshaweb/owadisp.show_document?p_table=OSHACT&p_id=3359

OSHA: OSHA Training Courses, Materials, and Resources. https://www.osha.gov/dte/index.html

OSHA: Permissible Exposure Limits (PELs).
http://www.osha.gov/dsg/topics/pel/index.html

OSHA: Quick Card. Protect Yourself. Carbon Monoxide Poisoning. http://www.osha.gov/Publications/3282-10N-05-English-07-18-2007.html

OSHA: Stairways and Ladders: A Guide to OSHA Rules. http://www.osha.gov/Publications/osha3124.pdf

OSHA: Wood Dust.
http://www.osha.gov/SLTC/wooddust/index.html

Sheet Metal and Air-Conditioning Contractors National Association (SMACNA): IAQ Guidelines for Occupied Buildings Under Construction, 2nd Edition. 2007. ASNI/SMACNA 008-2008. http://smacna.org/store

Section 4

Master Verification Checklist

The core technical component of Energy Savings Plus Health: IAQ Guidelines for School Building Upgrades is:

Section 2: Assessment Protocols and Recommended Actions.

Section 3 contains appendices that are referenced throughout the Guide.

Section 4 contains a Master Verification Checklist to help verify that the assessment protocols in Section 2 have been applied and that the appropriate actions to protect or enhance IAQ have been taken during the building upgrades. The checklist is a valuable tool for keeping track of progress during the building upgrade, including accomplishments and upcoming issues to be addressed.

Alternatively, the "Energy Saving Plus Health Checklist Generator" tool can be used to develop a custom verification checklist, along with the specific assessment protocols and recommended actions,

tailored to the building upgrade project. When using the Energy Saving Plus Health Checklist Generator it may be necessary to enable macros for functionality, depending on the users' Excel settings.

Use the "*Energy Saving Plus Health Checklist Generator*" To Create Your Custom Verification Checklist, Assessment Protocols and Recommended Actions

---

Note

All checklists are complementary to the material presented in Section 2 and should be used in conjunction with the assessment protocols and recommended actions. Section 2 should be thoroughly reviewed before verifying the protocols and recommended actions on the checklists.

Energy Savings Plus Health:

Indoor Air Quality Guidelines for School Building Upgrades Master Verification Checklist

United States Environmental Protection Agency

Note: This Verification Checklist is to be used in conjunction with the assessment protocols and recommended actions in Section 2 of *Energy Savings Plus Health: Indoor Air Quality Guidelines for School Building Upgrades.*

School Name/Building:

City/State/Zip: **Date:**

Assessment Protocol and Action Verification		Complete	N/A	NOTES
1.0 Project Planning/Integrated Design				
AP 1.1	Gathered feedback from the school's faculty and staff on IAQ issues and gained an understanding of the current building status. Conducted stakeholder meetings early in the design process.			
AP 1.2	Performed a building walkthrough inspection to identify IAQ issues and concerns.			
AP 1.3	Defined overall project IAQ and energy goals within the context of project scope and budget. Developed a communications plan with a clear process for addressing occupant concerns.			
AP 1.4	Selected a project team with IAQ expertise. Included a representative from each group of stakeholders in the building, for example, teachers, administrators, nurses, maintenance staff, parents and students. When evaluating proposals, ensured the project's IAQ and energy efficiency requirements are met and specific provisions for protecting IAQ during construction phases are included. See Appendix A for guidance on team selection.			
MA 1.1	Conducted collaborative cross-functional team meetings to identify synergies between IAQ and energy-efficiency upgrades. For large projects, held a Design Charrette with design professionals and representatives from the school, including IAQ coordinators, risk managers, administrators, teachers, nurses, and operations and maintenance staff.			
MA 1.2	Formalized project goals after collaborative design meetings. Clearly defined all IAQ and energy efficiency goals.			
MA 1.3	Finalized a project team with IAQ expertise. Designated representative(s) from the school's operations and maintenance staff to attend all team meetings.			
MA 1.4	Held regular meetings throughout design and construction to discuss project progress, synergies and challenges. Regularly communicated project plans and progress with stakeholders and responded to concerns.			

Color Codes   Assessment Protocol (AP)

1.0 Project Planning/Integrated Design (continued)

Assessment Protocol and Action Verification	Complete	N/A	NOTES
MA 1.5 Held a construction kick-off meeting with the design team, general contractor and site managers for each trade before construction begins. Continued meetings during construction process, with updates to stakeholders. Ensured the plan for protecting students and other occupants during the construction phases is adequately communicated.			
2.0 Commissioning			
AP 2.1 Determined which kind(s) of commissioning are appropriate (new system commissioning, recommissioning or retro-commissioning).			
MA 2.1 Designated and/or hired a Commissioning Agent, as appropriate for the project.			
MA 2.2 Developed an Owner's Project Requirements document, including formalized project goals, per MA 1.2. Clearly defined all IAQ and energy efficiency goals.			
MA 2.3 Developed a Basis of Design document to outline how the design will meet the Owner's Project Requirements.			
MA 2.4 Developed a Commissioning Plan, including an outline of commissioning activities, a schedule, a list of systems to be commissioned, and specifications to be included in the commissioning process.			
MA 2.5 Commissioned systems per the schedule outlined in the Commissioning Plan created for MA 2.4.			
MA 2.6 Delivered a third-party commissioning report to the facility manager (if a third-party Commissioning Agent was hired to perform commissioning activities).			
MA 2.7 Performed post-occupancy commissioning (as required).			
MA 2.8 Engaged the Commissioning Agent to train the facility manager and other operations and maintenance staff on all commissioned systems.			
EA 2.1 Included measurement and verification devices in the project design.			
EA 2.2 Developed a plan for recommissioning existing systems in the future as they age to ensure long-term system optimization.			
EA 2.3 Conducted follow-up training to reinforce operator skills and knowledge.			

Color Codes   Assessment Protocol (AP)

3.0 Moisture Control and Mold

Assessment Protocol and Action Verification		Complete	N/A	NOTES
AP 3.1	Inspected the interior and exterior of the building and the building's mechanical systems for evidence of moisture problems, and documented the results.			
AP 3.2	Determined whether the project requires mold remediation or additional moisture control measures based on the findings of the moisture inspection recommended in AP 3.1 or the IAQ walkthrough inspection recommended in AP 1.2.			
AP 3.3	Worked with a general contractor or other experienced building experts to define the scope of moisture improvements and repairs.			
AP 3.4	Assessed moisture or mold problems that could not be resolved under the project. Did not start construction projects that would reduce the school's air infiltration rate if there are unresolved moisture problems.			
MA 3.1	Repaired moisture problems identified during the assessment including plumbing leaks, rain leaks, and foundation leaks.			
MA 3.2	Conducted mold remediation following professional guidance, such as EPA's Mold Remediation In Schools And Commercial Buildings and IICRC Mold Remediation Standard S520.			
MA 3.3	Addressed standing water problems. Corrected surface water pooling near the foundation before insulating basement or crawlspace walls.			
MA 3.4	Managed rainwater in assemblies included within the scope of work (e.g., drainage planes and flashings). Ensured there is adequate slope and drainage away from the building.			
MA 3.5	Ensured proper HVAC condensate drainage. Ensured drain pans meet requirements of ASHRAE Standard 62.1.			
MA 3.6	Prevented condensation in the building by air sealing the enclosure, managing water vapor flow, managing air pressure relationships, ensuring all piping and valves with condensation potential are adequately insulated, and controlling indoor humidity sources.			
MA 3.7	Properly sized the HVAC system to manage moisture inside the building. Ensured that classroom HVAC systems provide continuous humidity control and maintain indoor relative humidity below 60%, ideally between 30% and 50%, if possible. Ensured proper indoor humidity control during summer months. If there is a school building summer shutdown program, ensured controls and HVAC operation are specified to keep indoor relative humidity within acceptable limits. Ensured regularly scheduled maintenance of humidification equipment. For mechanically ventilated buildings, ensured that the building meets the exfiltration requirements of ASHRAE Standard 62.1.			
MA 3.8	Used nonporous construction materials in moisture-prone areas.			

Color Codes

Assessment Protocol (AP)

3.0 Moisture Control and Mold (continued)

	Assessment Protocol and Action Verification	Complete	N/A	NOTES
MA 3.9	Protected open roof areas from rain during construction and designed and constructed roofing systems and flashing details to ensure proper moisture barriers. Repaired leaks before air sealing or insulating the attic.			
MA 3.10	Protected construction materials from moisture damage and did not use materials showing visible signs of mold or other biological growth. Stored and installed all building products, systems and components in strict accordance with manufacturers' printed instructions.			
EA 3.1	Retrofitted crawlspaces so that they are sealed, insulated, ventilated with conditioned air, properly drained and waterproofed. Installed a high-capacity, energy-efficient dehumidifier in the space (if climate conditions warranted).			
EA 3.2	Followed EPA or other professional guidance to perform additional activities to remediate any mold growth.			
EA 3.3	Considered ventilation approaches for better moisture control, including dedicated outdoor air systems (DOAS) and variable-air-volume (VAV) systems.			
4.0 Asbestos				
AP 4.1	Determined areas of the school that have already been identified as containing asbestos by reviewing the school's Asbestos Hazard Emergency Response Act (AHERA) asbestos management plan.			
AP 4.2	Inspected the building for asbestos-containing material (ACM) or, for new construction, verified that no asbestos was used in the building materials. If the school does not have an asbestos management plan and asbestos-containing materials are present, prepared an asbestos management plan.			
MA 4.1	Evaluated the condition of ACM. Immediately isolated the area if suspected ACM was found to be damaged (e.g., unraveling, frayed, breaking apart) and contacted an accredited and properly trained asbestos professional for abatement or repair.			
MA 4.2	Exercised caution to prevent the release of asbestos particles into the air during work activities (e.g., no dusting, sweeping or vacuuming ACM debris; no sawing, sanding, scraping, or drilling holes into ACM; no using abrasive pads or brushes to strip ACM).			
MA 4.3	Did not remove or disturb insulation that appears to be vermiculite.			
MA 4.4	Conducted asbestos abatement before blower door testing and exercised caution when conducting blower door testing where friable asbestos or vermiculite attic insulation is present (e.g., positively-pressurized blower door testing).			
MA 4.5	Conducted asbestos clearance air monitoring following any asbestos response actions in the school to ensure the actions were conducted properly, using a trained and accredited asbestos professional.			

Color Codes   Assessment Protocol (AP)

	5.0 Lead	Complete	N/A	NOTES
Assessment Protocol and Action Verification				
AP 5.1	Assumed lead-based paint was used in schools built before 1978, unless testing shows otherwise. Recognized that lead-based paint may be present in any school. Determined which painted surfaces will be disturbed during the planned work.			
AP 5.2	Tested any suspected surfaces that will be disturbed during the building upgrade. Paint samples may be taken and analyzed by an EPA-accredited laboratory, or an EPA-certified inspector or risk assessor may test paint via X-ray fluorescence [XRF] testing or, in some cases, a certified individual may use an EPA-recognized test kit.			
MA 5.1	Complied with EPA's Renovation, Repair and Painting (RRP) Program Rule (used a Certified Renovator, followed lead-safe work practices, isolated the work area to avoid occupant exposure, minimized lead dust, left no dust or debris behind, and successfully performed cleaning verification or clearance testing.).			
MA 5.2	Complied with all local and state regulations applicable to lead and hazard reduction activities.			
EA 5.1	Followed additional lead-safe rehabilitation practices in addition to EPA's RRP.			
EA 5.2	Replaced windows that test positive for lead-based paint.			
EA 5.3	Ensured all future paint applications in the school are lead-free.			
6.0 Polychlorinated Biphenyls (PCBs)				
AP 6.1	Determined whether fluorescent light ballasts containing polychlorinated biphenyls (PCBs) are present.			
AP 6.2	Assessed whether caulk will be disturbed during building upgrade activities.			
MA 6.1	Replaced PCB-containing fluorescent light ballasts that are leaking with new lighting fixtures. Any oil or stains leaked from PCB-containing ballasts were properly cleaned up or disposed of. Considered replacement of all PCB-containing light ballasts with new lighting fixtures.			
MA 6.2	Properly disposed of PCB-containing light ballasts and fluorescent bulbs containing mercury. Adhered to requirements of 40 CFR Part 761 Subpart D to ensure that any PCB-containing waste was handled properly.			
MA 6.3	If PCBs were potentially present in caulk that was disturbed during building renovations, took steps to minimize exposure following EPA's Current Best Practices for PCBs in Caulk. Adhered to requirements of 40 CFR Part 761 Subpart D to ensure that any PCB-containing waste was handled properly. Documented and stored copies of all test results and all disposal measures.			
EA 6.1	If there are additional concerns about PCBs, conducted an assessment for PCBs in indoor air following EPA's Compendium Method TO-4A (high air volume) or Compendium Method TO-10A (low air volume). If air quality tests indicated concentrations above EPA's Public Health Levels for PCBs in Indoor School Air, identified potential sources of PCBs and mitigation options. Adhered to requirements of 40 CFR Part 761 Subpart D to ensure that any PCB-containing waste was handled properly. Documented and stored copies of all test results and all disposal measures.			

Color Codes   Assessment Protocol (AP)

7.0 Radon

Assessment Protocol and Action Verification		Complete	N/A	NOTES
AP 7.1	Selected a radon testing professional from a list of qualified testers obtained from the state radon office. If there are no state requirements, selected a radon professional who is trained or certified by the American Association of Radon Scientists & Technologists, Inc. (AARST) National Radon Proficiency Program or the National Radon Safety Board (NRSB).			
AP 7.2	Performed radon testing before school building modifications in accordance with applicable state requirements or other guidance, such as the ANSI/AARST Radon Measurement in Schools and Large Buildings standard.			
AP 7.3	Retested for radon after completion of all building upgrades and renovations that affect building envelope leakage and airflows.			
MA 7.1	Mitigated high radon levels. Took actions to reduce radon levels as outlined in the ASNI/AARST Radon Mitigation in Schools and Large Buildings standard, using active soil depressurization as the first mitigation method considered, if radon levels are equal to or greater than 4 pCi/L, before or after building modifications.			
MA 7.2	Ensured school HVAC systems are operating properly, with outdoor air ventilation maintained at or above design minimum values.			
MA 7.3	Advised periodic retesting of areas in the school that have been mitigated for radon.			
8.0 Belowground Vapor-Forming Contaminants (Except Radon)				
AP 8.1	Evaluated potential sources and odors (e.g., gasoline, sewer gas or fuel oil).			
AP 8.2	Evaluated the sewer vent system to confirm that drain traps have water in them and inspected drain lines for breaks or leaks.			
AP 8.3	Notified local or state authorities and pursued additional assessments before continuing project work in the event an odor source could not be identified, and the building is in a known area of contamination.			
AP 8.4	Conducted a further assessment if vapor-forming soil or groundwater contamination is suspected on or near the building site. Consulted state or tribal voluntary brownfields cleanup programs or environmental regulatory agencies for information on the risks of vapor intrusion.			
MA 8.1	Repaired or replaced failed or unattached sewer vent system components before proceeding with energy projects.			
MA 8.2	Addressed drain traps prone to drying out by developing a maintenance plan to periodically add water to the traps, and considered installation of inline drain seals to floor drains prone to drying out.			

Color Codes   Assessment Protocol (AP)

8.0 Belowground Vapor-Forming Contaminants (Except Radon) (continued)			
Assessment Protocol and Action Verification	Complete	N/A	NOTES
MA 8.3	Assessed and mitigated soil gas vapor intrusion in compliance with local or state standards (Table X5.1 of ASTM E2600 or EPA guidance).			
EA 8.1	Installed floor drain seals to untrapped floor drains.			
EA 8.2	Installed automatic drain trap primers in floor drains that are susceptible to drying out to ensure that a small amount of water is periodically delivered to the trap and to prevent it from drying out.			
EA 8.3	Implemented the proper measures to prevent migration of soil-gas contaminants into occupied spaces for new construction and building expansion projects located on brownfield sites, as described in ASHRAE IAQ Guide, Strategy 3.4.			
9.0 Vehicle Exhaust			
AP 9.1	Investigated complaints regarding motor vehicle exhaust emissions. Requested feedback from the school nurse, facilities staff and the school's IAQ coordinator and determined the locations and dates of complaints.			
AP 9.2	Identified locations of air leaks from parking structures to occupied spaces.			
AP 9.3	Identified locations of outdoor air intake vents and assessed whether they are located an adequate distance away from areas where vehicles may idle.			
MA 9.1	Followed local and state anti-idling laws and policies. Otherwise, established and enforced a requirement that all engines must be shut off (no idle zone) at loading docks and vehicle loading and unloading zones. Provided signage to designate the limits of no idle zones.			
MA 9.2	Sealed locations that separate parking structures from occupied spaces. Air sealed leaks into ceiling cavities, windows and doors; electrical, plumbing and duct penetrations; cracks between masonry or concrete walls and unsealed penetrations; and leaks in the duct work or air handler platforms.			
MA 9.3	Maintained occupied spaces near parking structures at a positive pressure relative to the parking structures.			
MA 9.4	Decoupled areas with vehicle exhaust emissions from building air handling systems. Eliminated and disconnected supply diffusers and return grilles in garages and vocational classrooms from air handling systems that serve other occupied spaces.			
MA 9.5	Specified carbon monoxide (CO) detection and warning equipment in accordance with NFPA 720 and any applicable local or state requirements.			

Color Codes

Assessment Protocol (AP)

9.0 Vehicle Exhaust (continued)

Assessment Protocol and Action Verification	Complete	N/A	NOTES
MA 9.6 Ensured that new outdoor air intakes meet the ASHRAE Standard 62.1, Table 5.5.1 separation distance requirements from any sources of vehicular emissions.			
MA 9.7 Protected existing outdoor air intakes if they did not meet the ASHRAE Standard 62.1, Table 5.5.1 separation distance requirements by relocating them or relocating emissions source locations.			
MA 9.8 Properly installed a supplemental vented heating system in the parking structure (if needed).			
EA 9.1 If feasible, relocated existing outdoor air intakes away from vehicle exhaust sources to avoid entrainment.			
EA 9.2 Installed particle filtration, and in extreme cases gas-phase air cleaning devices, to treat ventilation air for outdoor pollutants (see EA 19.1).			
EA 9.3 Added a positive pressure vestibule at all doorways connected to parking areas, to provide an airlock between parking structures and occupied spaces.			
EA 9.4 Installed or upgraded exhaust systems for enclosed parking areas that provide adequate exhaust for all localized sources of contamination; maintain sealed exhaust ductwork in plenum spaces under a negative pressure; and exhaust to the outdoors, meeting the minimum separation distance requirements of ASHRAE Standard 62.1, Table 5.5.1.			

10.0 Local and Regional Ambient Air Quality

Assessment Protocol and Action Verification	Complete	N/A	NOTES
AP 10.1 Investigated published information regarding local sources of pollution and regional outdoor air quality, including outdoor ozone levels.			
MA 10.1 In areas where national standards for outdoor particulate matter or ozone are exceeded, ensured that mechanical ventilation systems are designed and operated to meet the outdoor air filtration and air cleaning requirements of ASHRAE Standard 62.1, Section 6.2.1.			
EA 10.1 In addition to the requirements of MA 10.1, in areas where national standards for outdoor particulate matter or ozone are exceeded, ensured that mechanical ventilation systems are designed and operated to meet the outdoor air filtration and air cleaning requirements of ASHRAE Standard 189.1, Section 8.3.1.3.			

11.0 Pests

Assessment Protocol and Action Verification	Complete	N/A	NOTES
AP 11.1 Identified potential pests of concern, including any organisms likely to colonize the building based on project location.			
AP 11.2 Identified evidence of pests, and determined whether pesticides are being used in the building to control pest populations.			

Color Codes

Assessment Protocol (AP)

	Assessment Protocol and Action Verification	Complete	N/A	NOTES
11.0 Pests (continued)				
AP 11.3	Assessed whether the school already has an Integrated Pest Management (IPM) plan and whether it is being followed and sustained.			
MA 11.1	Selected a third-party certified IPM professional for pest management needs. Determined whether pesticides will need to be used. Considered providing signage to communicate when pesticide applications will occur. Encouraged scheduling pesticide applications when school is not in session.			
MA 11.2	Patched and sealed openings in areas with evidence of rodent infestation, with rodent-resistant materials prior to installing weatherization materials that may be susceptible to gnawing.			
MA 11.3	Reduced the potential for pest entry into the building by blocking, sealing and eliminating pest entry points around the building envelope.			
MA 11.4	Reduced the risk of pest dispersal throughout the building by sealing and blocking interior passageways.			
MA 11.5	Implemented protections for outdoor air intakes and exhausts to eliminate pest entryways.			
MA 11.6	Maintained existing pest protections within the building.			
MA 11.7	Removed clutter, eliminated wood piles and waste near the building, and removed any bushes, trees or vegetation closer than two feet from the structure. Kept vegetation away from outdoor air intakes and outdoor mechanical equipment. Did not pile up soils and mulches against the building's exterior walls.			
MA 11.8	Ensured the school has an IPM plan, and it is being followed prior to pesticide applications.			
EA 11.1	Ensured all exterior garbage cans and dumpsters are sealable and sanitized regularly.			
EA 11.2	Followed guidance for institutional kitchens in the SF Environment document "Pest Prevention by Design."			
12.0 Tracked-In Pollutants				
AP 12.1	Inspected all building entrances for walk-off mats or entry mat systems. Noted conditions of dirt or moisture accumulation near entrances that might need walk-off mats or entryway floor cleaning systems.			
MA 12.1	Provided walk-off mats to trap dirt and moisture at all building entrances.			
MA 12.2	Followed EPA's Building and Grounds Maintenance Checklist and provided a copy to the facility manager.			
EA 12.1	Installed permanent entryway systems at all regularly used building entrances to capture dirt and particulates in accordance with ASHRAE Standard 189.1, Section 8.3.1.5, or EPA's IAQ Design Tools for Schools, Entry Mat Barriers.			

Color Codes   Assessment Protocol (AP)

13.0 Building Products/Materials Emissions

Assessment Protocol and Action Verification	Complete	N/A	NOTES
AP 13.1 Reviewed content and emissions documentation for products and materials being considered for the project to determine whether they contain potentially hazardous compounds.			
MA 13.1 Selected the least toxic products or materials feasible for each application. Used products and materials that indicate they have (or are certified as having) low VOC content or low VOC emissions. Specified products and materials that meet independent certification and testing protocols (see examples listed in MA 13.1).			
MA 13.2 Selected low-emitting wood and composite-wood products compliant with California Title 17 ATCM. (If CA Title 17 ATCM compliant materials are not available, used wood products that meet Section 6.1 of EPA's Indoor airPLUS Construction Specifications.)			
MA 13.3 Ensured the school meets the Minimum Actions in Priority Issues 19.0 Outdoor Air Ventilation and 20.0 Exhaust Ventilation.			
MA 13.4 Performed a post-construction building flush-out in the renovated building/spaces before occupancy resumes.			
MA 13.5 Followed guidance outlined in MA 22.3 to protect absorptive materials during construction.			
MA 13.6 Followed Priority Issue 22.0 Protecting IAQ During Construction to protect children and other occupants.			
EA 13.1 Aired out new construction materials in a well-ventilated, clean and dry space prior to installation.			
EA 13.2 Sealed composite wood products with a low-VOC or no-VOC sealant intended to reduce VOC emissions.			
EA 13.3 Investigated and corrected potential contaminant source problems after building modifications.			
EA 13.4 Performed a post-construction flush-out or baseline IAQ monitoring per ASHRAE Standard 189.1, Section 10.3.1.4(b) after construction was completed.			
EA 13.5 Required products that have submitted their complete chemical inventory to a third party for verification. Made the verification / certification by the third party publicly available.			

14.0 Vented Combustion Appliances

	Complete	N/A	NOTES
AP 14.1 Completed a safety inspection of all vented combustion appliances in the school.			
MA 14.1 Completed all applicable actions under the Assessment Protocols (AP 14.1) and repaired, removed or replaced combustion appliances to correct deficiencies and ensure compliance with applicable codes and standards. Ensured proper venting after modifications that affect building envelope leakage and airflows.			

Color Codes   Assessment Protocol (AP)

14.0 Vented Combustion Appliances (continued)

Assessment Protocol and Action Verification		Complete	N/A	NOTES
MA 14.2	Ensured that all combustion exhaust is captured as close to the combustion source as possible, exhausted directly outdoors, and not vented into other indoor spaces such as attics, crawlspaces or basements.			
MA 14.3	Ensured that vented appliances have sufficient makeup air to replace vented air and maintain normal operating conditions.			
MA 14.4	Ensured that boiler firing adjustments are operating properly.			
MA 14.5	Verified proper installation of CO detection and warning equipment to meet the requirements of NFPA 720 and any applicable local or state requirements.			
EA 14.1	Installed power vented or sealed combustion equipment when replacing combustion equipment located in occupied or conditioned spaces. Installation was performed in accordance with ACCA Standard 5.			

15.0 Unvented Combustion Appliances

		Complete	N/A	NOTES
AP 15.1	Identified unvented combustion appliances and determined whether any local or state regulations prohibiting these devices apply.			
MA 15.1	Ensured adequate ventilation and exhaust in spaces with unvented combustion equipment. Ensured ASHRAE Standard 62.1 requirements for outdoor air ventilation and exhaust are met for each specific room where unvented combustion equipment is used (e.g., food prep areas, science labs). Ensured rooms where CO is likely to be generated are operated at a negative pressure relative to surrounding areas. Ensured that negative pressures in kitchens induced by exhaust fans do not exceed NFPA 96 Section 8.2.1 guidelines due to a lack of make-up air.			
MA 15.2	With the school's permission, removed all unvented combustion space heaters (e.g., unvented gas or kerosene space heaters) that do not conform to local or state regulations.			
MA 15.3	Verified proper installation of CO detection and warning equipment meeting the requirements of NFPA 720 and any applicable local or state requirements.			

16.0 Ozone From Indoor Sources

		Complete	N/A	NOTES
AP 16.1	Identified indoor sources of ozone and determined whether any air-cleaning or purifying equipment designed to intentionally produce ozone was present.			
MA 16.1	Did not install any air cleaning equipment designed to intentionally produce ozone. Recommended removal of existing air cleaning equipment designed to intentionally produce ozone.			

Color Codes

Assessment Protocol (AP)

16.0 Ozone From Indoor Sources (continued)			
Assessment Protocol and Action Verification	Complete	N/A	NOTES
MA 16.2 Ensured adequate ventilation and exhaust in areas with ozone-generating office equipment, including printing, copying and reprographics rooms.			
EA 16.1 Tested office equipment for ozone emissions following ASTM D6670-01. Repaired or removed equipment if emissions exceeded 0.02 mg/m³.			
EA 16.2 Installed office equipment fitted with ozone capture / removal systems.			
17.0 Environmental Tobacco Smoke			
AP 17.1 Assessed school smoking policy and determined whether the school has a policy that prohibits smoking inside the school. Determined whether there are locations on school grounds where outdoor smoking may be allowed, and the locations of these locations from the building's entrances, outdoor air intakes and operable windows.			
AP 17.2 Identified whether there have been occupant complaints about smoking.			
MA 17.1 Ensured that the school has a policy on tobacco that is consistent with local, state and federal laws. The policy should include prohibitions against tobacco use by students, all school staff, parents, and visitors on school property, in school vehicles, and at school-sponsored functions away from school property. Ensured any locations where outdoor smoking is permitted are a minimum of 25 feet from all building entrances, outdoor air intakes and operable windows.			
18.0 HVAC Equipment			
AP 18.1 Conducted an HVAC assessment to evaluate the condition of the existing HVAC system components in accordance with minimum inspection standards of ASHRAE/ACCA Standard 180, ASHRAE handbooks or other equivalent standards and guidelines. Evaluated building heating and cooling loads after planned modifications and HVAC equipment capacities for sensible and latent loads.			
MA 18.1 Repaired, modified or replaced equipment to ensure that existing HVAC systems operate properly. Ensured there is a scheduled inspection and maintenance program for HVAC systems in accordance with ASHRAE/ACCA Standard 180.			
MA 18.2 Properly sized and installed any new HVAC equipment.			
MA 18.3 Ensured any new HVAC systems have a minimum of MERV 8 filters installed upstream of all cooling coils and wetted surfaces, in accordance with ASHRAE Standard 62.1 requirements.			
MA 18.4 Remediated mold in air plenums and ductwork, following guidance outlined in MA 3.2.			
MA 18.5 Followed the guidelines in the OSHA Technical Manual: Legionnaires' Disease to protect against bacterial growth in HVAC systems and mechanical equipment.			

Color Codes   Assessment Protocol (AP)

18.0 HVAC Equipment (continued)	Complete	N/A	NOTES
Assessment Protocol and Action Verification			
EA 18.1	Installed higher efficiency filters in any new HVAC systems (MERV 11 or higher), upstream of all cooling coils and wetted surfaces, if feasible.			
EA 18.2	Increased filter efficiencies in existing HVAC systems (highest MERV rating possible based on equipment specifications).			
EA 18.3	Employed filtration and gas-phase air cleaning strategies to further improve IAQ, in conjunction with source control strategies and maintaining minimum ventilation rates.			
19.0 Outdoor Air Ventilation			
AP 19.1	Determined whether HVAC systems comply with ASHRAE Standard 62.1 ventilation requirements at the system level and in the breathing zones of all occupied spaces.			
MA 19.1	Adjusted existing HVAC systems to meet all requirements of ASHRAE Standard 62.1, where possible, using the Ventilation Rate Procedure.			
MA 19.2	Considered the impacts of building envelope air sealing on ventilation. Avoided tightening the building shell and reducing air exchange rates if increasing ventilation or installing additional ventilation is not possible. Ensured school buildings that rely on natural ventilation have adequate ventilation after weatherization.			
MA 19.3	Designed and installed new HVAC systems to meet all ventilation requirements of ASHRAE Standard 62.1 using the Ventilation Rate Procedure.			
MA 19.4	Verified that all HVAC systems meet any local code requirements for ventilation.			
EA 19.1	Replaced or upgraded existing HVAC systems to meet ASHRAE Standard 62.1.			
EA 19.2	For mechanical ventilation applications, installed permanent outdoor airflow monitoring systems in accordance with ASHRAE Standard 189.1, Section 8.3.1.2. For natural ventilation applications, provided monitoring to ensure operable windows and other ventilation openings are operated appropriately to ensure adequate ventilation.			
EA 19.3	Applied advanced ventilation approaches, such as dedicated outdoor air systems (DOAS), demand-controlled ventilation, displacement ventilation, economizers, energy recovery ventilation, and variable-air-volume (VAV) systems. Ensured ASHRAE Standard 62.1 ventilation requirements are met for all loads and occupancy conditions.			
EA 19.4	Implemented pre-occupancy ventilation control for ventilation systems that serve spaces that are not continuously occupied, to provide the design minimum outdoor air ventilation rate for a period of one hour prior to expected occupancy whenever the spaces have been unventilated for a period longer than 24 hours.			

Color Codes

Assessment Protocol (AP)

20.0 Exhaust Ventilation

Assessment Protocol and Action Verification	Complete	N/A	NOTES
AP 20.1 Identified rooms or areas with localized contaminant sources that require exhaust ventilation.			
AP 20.2 Measured exhaust airflows to determine whether there is compliance with the exhaust requirements of ASHRAE Standard 62.1 for each space.			
AP 20.3 Verified that exhaust from rooms with localized contaminant sources discharge outdoors and do not discharge or leak into other indoor spaces or the building structure.			
MA 20.1 Ensured exhaust is provided for rooms or areas with localized indoor contaminant sources as identified in AP 20.1 and ensured that exhaust rates required by ASHRAE Standard 62.1 are met.			
MA 20.2 Confirmed proper functionality of the exhaust systems to reduce causes of complaints.			
EA 20.1 Implemented additional efforts to prevent the recirculation of exhausted air into outdoor air intakes.			
EA 20.2 Provided monitoring and alarms for exhaust systems.			

21.0 Building Safety for Children and Other Occupants

Assessment Protocol and Action Verification	Complete	N/A	NOTES
AP 21.1 Identified the School's Health and Safety Officer or Committee and included them in all building safety planning. Documented safety hazards that were observed during the assessments. *Immediately responded to urgent and life-threatening situations.* Ensured the results of the safety assessment were provided to the school's health and safety representatives, and corrective actions are considered as part of building upgrades.			
AP 21.2 Assessed the proper functionality of fire alarms, smoke alarms, and CO detection and warning equipment. Determined whether CO detection and warning equipment meets the requirements of NFPA 720 and applicable local and state requirements.			
AP 21.3 Identified the prevalence of harmful chemicals in accessible locations, including custodial closets, storage areas under sinks, science labs, hospitality training programs, art labs, food labs and vocational programs.			
AP 21.4 Identified risk of mercury exposure in existing school lighting, equipment (e.g., thermometers, barometers), components and lab supplies. Determined whether the school has a mercury spill response plan.			
AP 21.5 Identified the locations of fire extinguishers in the school, and verified that all placements meet local laws.			
AP 21.6 Determined whether the hot water heater temperature setting is within the allowable limits of the local and state codes.			
MA 21.1 *Immediately corrected life-threatening safety risks.* Corrected other safety hazards during the building upgrades.			

Color Codes   Assessment Protocol (AP)

21.0 Building Safety for Children and Other Occupants (continued)

Assessment Protocol and Action Verification		Complete	N/A	NOTES
MA 21.2	Had qualified personnel correct deficiencies with fire alarms, smoke alarms or CO detection and warning equipment. Installed additional fire alarms, smoke alarms and CO detection and warning equipment wherever necessary.			
MA 21.3	Ensured appropriate storage of hazardous chemicals.			
MA 21.4	Prevented mercury exposure by ensuring school has a mercury spill response plan. Prevented mercury spills by removing all elemental mercury, mercury compounds and mercury-containing equipment. Properly disposed of all elementary mercury supplies and mercury containing devices and equipment, including fluorescent lighting, compact fluorescent light (CFL) bulbs and mercury-containing thermostats.			
MA 21.5	Corrected deficiencies associated with fire extinguishers.			
MA 21.6	Adjusted water heater temperatures to prevent scalding.			
EA 21.1	Installed enhanced CO detection and warning equipment that can detect and store low peak CO levels, and considered integration with the building's central monitoring system.			
EA 21.2	Installed light switches at the top and bottom of all stairwells.			
EA 21.3	Installed safety lighting on or near steps.			
EA 21.4	Repaired malfunctioning doors, windows, roofs and floors.			
EA 21.5	Qualified personnel ensured the safety of electrical systems by confirming they are in accordance with applicable codes.			
22.0 Protecting IAQ During Construction				
AP 22.1	Determined building occupancy patterns during expected construction periods, and identified any anticipated special needs of the building occupants.			
AP 22.2	Identified potential construction-related contaminants and the pathways through which they could impact the IAQ of building occupants.			
MA 22.1	Minimized occupant and worker exposures during construction (e.g., adhered to SMACNA Indoor Air Quality Guidelines for Occupied Buildings under Construction). Properly isolated work areas from occupants. Promptly responded to any occupant complaints or concerns.			
MA 22.2	Protected HVAC systems from contaminants during work activities, performed post-construction inspections. Cleaned to remove dust and debris from ductwork, as needed. Ensured new HVAC filters were installed prior to occupancy.			
MA 22.3	Protected highly absorptive materials from airborne contaminants and emissions caused by construction.			

Color Codes   Assessment Protocol (AP)

22.0 Protecting IAQ During Construction (continued)

Assessment Protocol and Action Verification	Complete	N/A	NOTES
MA 22.4 Safely installed spray foam insulation and employed safe work practices to avoid exposure to spray polyurethane foam (SPF).			
EA 22.1 Considered and implemented additional protections as appropriate and necessary to protect the health and safety of building occupants.			

23.0 Jobsite Safety

	Complete	N/A	NOTES
AP 23.1 Evaluated existing and potential health concerns and activities. Referred to Appendix C: Worker Protection for recommended evaluation measures and actions.			
MA 23.1 Referred to Appendix C: Worker Protection for recommended actions to protect worker safety.			

Color Codes   Assessment Protocol (AP)   Minimum Action (MA)   Expanded Action (EA)